Contents

Modern Conceptions of Human Transmission

Saying the Unsayable – The Science of Subconscious Signaling

Seeing is Believing – How to Pinpoint The Top 14 Body Language Profiles

Key Gestures that Change The Game – How to Analyze & Capitalize

The Telepath – How to Read, *Mine* & Hijack the Mind

The Gateway – Opening your Pineal Gland for Psychiatric Power

Easy, Everyday Techniques for Awakening Your Inner Eye

Gearing Up: Top Ways to PREPARE your Personal

Psychological Warfare

Brain Freeze- Knowing WHEN to Permeate the Psyche

World Dominance – How to ALWAYS Send the Correct Cultural Signals

The Body of Power – Unleashing your Bioenergetics

A Special Note

Body Language MASTERED

How to Dominate Modern Life with Primal Powers

By C.K. Murray

Copyright © 2018 C.K. Murray

All Rights Reserved

Join the Newsletter

Similar works by C.K. Murray:

Master Mind: Unleashing the Infinite Power of the Latent Brain

Health Hacks - 46 Hacks to Improve Your Mood, Boost Your Performance, and Guarantee a Longer, Healthier, More Vibrant Life

MIND SHIFT - The Key to Erasing Negative Thoughts and Unlocking Positive Perception

Body Language Explained: How to Master the Power of the Unconscious

DOMINATE - How Psychopaths Think, Act and Succeed

DISCLAIMER

If you are uninformed or weak-minded, this book is not for you.

If you are *unprepared* to fully optimize a whole range of advanced body language secrets and strategies, this book is not for you.

If you are new to the scene, still unsure and uncertain, I advise you to read the prequel to this resource, "Body Language Explained: How to Master the Power of the Unconscious."

If, however, you are cognizant, careful and willing to go further, to plumb the hidden depths of *extra*ordinary body language, and to MASTER the shadows of the subconscious mind, then let us continue...

The following book will explore ancient truths you never thought you'd know.
In many ways, every thing you *thought* you knew, is about to change…

Prepare yourself.

                                Your Time Is Now

You'd be a *no*body without body language.

Fortunately, you and I and a whole host of others, are already there. Prepared, well ahead of the stragglers and looking to go further.

By now, you've read the books and know the basics. Body language is important. Nonverbal communication is important. Eyes peeled, mind ready. You see this, it might mean *that*. You observe one thing, it means another. You watch the way a person moves, talks, and navigates this world, and you learn. You understand, you react, and you maximize your chances of success.

Good - but what if that's not enough?

If you, like many in this maniacal modern world, are looking for more—then you know:

You've got *so* much left to learn...

Truth is, most body language books and primers are elementary. They are lacking, offering nonsensical stereotypical pop-culture pseudo-babble. These so-called 'explanations' are merely uninformed excuses for a phenomenon that is incredibly complex.

These books are *bunk*.
They oversimplify and they understate, and at the end of reading (or skimming) the un-enlightening pages, you feel like you've barely learned a thing.

Truth is, a lot of body language is intuitive. You already know it. You just don't know that you know it. And as for those potent nonverbal powers that you *don't* know?

Well, let's just put it this way: if you want something that is easy to apply, but lackluster in results, then read something else.

But if you want to *exponentially* increase your use, application, and power over the Subconscious Realm, stay right here. Because you're here for one thing...

Power. Not necessarily power over others, or even over your immediate surroundings. Maybe not even power over yourself. What you're looking for is Power of Potential. That is, the ability to know, without a shred, shadow, or modicum of doubt, that You. Can. Do it.

You want to have that power in your pocket, at all times. To feel as if you're <u>The One</u>. The person capable of dispensing incredible psychological powers on a whim. Capable of talking and interacting with anyone life throws your way. With family. With friends. With coworkers, and bosses, and important, significant actors that would have otherwise ruled *you*.

You want to have power that keeps you moving. Keeps you progressing. Keeps you confident and in control. You don't need to flaunt it, you don't even necessarily need others to know you have it.

But you want it. And from time to time, you want to unleash it in all its depth and breadth.

What you seek by reading this in-depth guide is the power to harness advanced body language in a way that is pivotal for turbocharging your life. For jumpstarting new connections and ideas. New relationships. Better jobs and careers. Happier and more exciting daily lives.

You want to take your life to the next level.

And by mastering the modern world of body language, you will.

Modern Conceptions of Human Transmission

Truth be told, body language is awesome.

But it is also extremely, undeniably dangerous. When you wield the full brunt of nonverbal communication, you are essentially applying an ancient tool. Like any tool, it can be used for good. To carve new pathways for growth and prosperity. To carry yourself and others toward a better place. To build a new future for yourself and those you hold closest.

But it can also be used for bad. To unearth deep, dark, disturbing secrets about the world. Secrets about people you didn't know. The things they say without saying. The minuscule nuances of their natures, the subtle signals that most people would never even notice…

If you use this gift for bad, you can do damage. You can weaponize body language against those you don't care for, even against those you love—when life leaves you vengeful.

And this is a problem. Why? Because body language is literally embedded in our beings. Because body language is an ingrained psycho-social facet of our existence... literally encoded in our ancestral and cultural DNA...

It is a part of us. It is not merely a part of us, it is physically inseparable from the lifeblood that sustains us.

If you choose to use your mastery of body language for evil, you are making a conscious choice to destroy that sacred bond. You are committing yourself to the darkest of forces.

In going forward, I will not tell you to not do so. I will merely caution you. Manipulation, deception, persuasion, coercion, and psychological warfare are all tactics we may apply, as sentient humans. They are all things that all of us, at one time or another, may opt to employ.

It is up to you how you choose to use them. You can do so sparingly, with respect for the gravity of the power. Or you can become warped by that power, controlling others like mere puppets on a string. At the end of the day, it's not about what you choose to do with your mastered powers... it's what you choose *not* to do.

Remember, restraint is a sign of true strength.

Sometimes in life, we don't need to use it. We merely need to show it.

Like a warrior with a blade in his sheath, or a soldier with a gun at his hip… Sometimes, merely letting others know what we can do is enough.

But I digress...

What matters moving forward is that you have what you need. You've already pieced together many of the building blocks of body language. You have a firm foundation. You have a vision. You have a conviction that burns within. Now, you just need to bring that passion to fruition.

It is time to optimize your understanding of body language, so that nobody can reign over you.
And that all starts with what truly makes this 'language' tick…

Saying the Unsayable – The Science of Subconscious Signaling

Think about body language for a second.

What it is? Seriously, do you know? You might think you know, you might even *think* you have a firm grasp of the various forms of nonverbal communication—but do you?

Have you ever truly, fully, considered what the term *body language* even means? What are its known forms and functions? What does it achieve? How do these various features compare and contrast?

Before we can delve into the life-changing uses and effects of body language, we must delve into what, exactly, this concept really is.

Consider the first thoughts that come to mind. You think of what you do with the body first, obviously. The way you walk and stand. Your posture, what you do with your arms and hands. The way you move your head. Now, consider your actual attributes. Your physical features. You have your eyes, your lips, your mouth—perhaps, your tongue? Then you've got what you wear. Are you dressed dapper or like a total hobo? Is there a certain brand you like to wear? A certain message conveyed through your shirt and pants? How about your hygiene? Your hair length, or color? Do you have tattoos or piercings? Do you wear earrings, or hats, or watches, or shoes, or other sorts of adornments? Do you use a certain cologne or perfume? How about your environment? How do you navigate that environment? Do you walk quietly and softly? Do you tread easy? Do you take bigger or smaller steps? Are you a louder walker? How do you occupy and navigate spaces? How do you use changes in your voice, in the frequency of your voice? Do you capitalize on silence, or do you keep a constant volume level? Do you spend a lot of time doing certain things, or are you noticeably quick and to-the-point?

All of the aforementioned things are considered part of nonverbal communication and body language. And they are powerful. Why? Because what we say is merely said. But what we don't say, is attributed to our innermost conscience. To what we *truly* think.

Look, you and I both know people say all kinds of things. They say they're happy when they're sad, say they're good when they're not, say they… love you when they don't? Point is, we all from time to time talk the talk. But do we walk the walk? Better question, is that 'walk' anything like that 'talk'?

In many cases, the answer is a resounding NO.

This is why understanding body language is so important. Even more, this is why mastering body language is critical. Do you realize how much of a leg-up, this level of proficiency, of excellence, can get you in the World? Not just in the business world, in corporate this or that, or for this career or that job, but in general.

A firm grasp of body language can get you way, way, way ahead of your competition. It can shoot you into the stratosphere. And the beauty? Many people won't even know how you did it. They'll be left wondering, and they'll just assume, that you have something they don't.

They're wrong!

We can all master body language. Sure, it comes more naturally to some. Some people are more intuitive, more sociable, more manipulative, more prone to leadership, and so on. But what matters is that we make the effort, the conscious effort, and that we make it work *unconsciously*.

So how do we do that?

Well first, we understand what body language is.
So what is it??

Well, to put it simply: body language is communication. But it's *not* simple. Sometimes it is; many times it is not. But it is, always, communication.

So what's communication?

Communication is the transmission of a message.
Now, some people will tell you that communication is only what you *intend* to transmit. This is false. This is patently false. After all, many times we say one thing and do another. Why? Because we don't want other people to know our true intentions, feelings, emotions and so on. So we lie, or we distort, or we spin white lies and half-truths, or we totally omit our underlying motives.

Communication is based on two things: sender and receiver.

When it comes to body language communication, whether it be what we physically do with our body, or something we have *on* our body, or in the way we verbalize with our body (tone of voice, pitch, accent, etc.), body language communication must always have a sender and a receiver. This is how a message is communicated. There can be multiple receivers and multiple senders. Or say, in the case of a concert, maybe just one sender and *thousands* of receivers.

But not all messages are received by *all* receivers.

Hypothetically, there is always a receiver. But some receivers never get the message. All you have to do is go to a local bar for the best example of this phenomenon. Just look at all the sexes intermingling. One woman might be trying to show a guy that she likes him by flashing her hair or stroking his shirt. She is transmitting the message that she finds him attractive.

He may or may not get this message. He may or may not be oblivious.

Similarly, one woman might be turning away, diverting her eyes, or trying to distance herself from a guy pursuing her. In this case, she is transmitting the message that she is not interested. He may or may not be getting this message.

Now, even if this guy continues to pursue, that does not mean he didn't receive the message. Perhaps, he thinks he can 'win' her over. Perhaps he simply doesn't care and is becoming aggressive. Or perhaps he has no idea, is sooo drunk, that he thinks every girl in the bar wants him like Brad Pitt...

Fact is, the sending and receiving of body language messages is not always easy to discern. It's even less easy to fully understand. Body language communication hinges on many factors, personal, interpersonal, environmental, psychological—you name it.

But…

It can be simplified.

According to most seminal scholars, there are essentially six types of body language communication:

(A) Intended Messages – 1) Not received   (2) Received
(3) Received Incorrectly
(B) Unintended Messages – 4) Not received   (5) Received
(6) Received Incorrectly

What this means can be explained simply. You can *intend* to send somebody a message, but they totally don't get it. Or they get it. Or they notice the body language behind it, but misinterpret what you intended.

Now, you can also *not* intend to send somebody a body language message. They can either not get it at all, get it (which you didn't intend), or get it partially but interpret it incorrectly.

Now, think of these six type of messages using the aforementioned bar scene scenario.

Okay.
So a female is flirting with a male. The female is unlikely to come right out and say, *"I want to sleep with you."* Now,

she might at a later point. But initially, she is going to show interest through body language. She can do this countless ways, obviously, but let's say her body language is to stroke her hair to highlight her femininity. Okay, so she's stroking her hair and sending the message that she is attracted to the male in question.

Now, let's go deeper. First, let's begin with intended messages. In this case, she is stroking her hair consciously. She wants the male to notice her, to find her attractive, to keep talking to her, etc. So she sends this message of attraction with intent, and now the male—the receiver—can do one of three things. If the message is *not* received, he may lose confidence and stop talking to her entirely. He may think she's not interested and continue talking to her, but simply in a friendly, non-sexual, fashion.

Okay, now let's say the male *does* receive her message of attraction. So what does he do? Well, he can send his own body language messages, perhaps by flexing, or arching his back, or coming closer, or talking deeper, or touching her. There are countless things he can do. Now, he can also do nothing. Say he receives the message, but doesn't want to reciprocate, not yet. Or say he likes talking to her but simply doesn't find her sexually attractive. Maybe he merely likes the conversation or her company. Even if he receives her message of attraction, he does not have to actively pursue her.

Now let's say he receives the message, but misinterprets it. So while there *is* communication, it is *mis*communication. In this case, the male sees her stroking her hair and thinks it means she's not interested. He thinks it means she is bored, and merely stroking her hair because she wants the conversation to end. He thinks the stroking of the hair is nothing more than an unconscious grooming. He thinks maybe she's a hairdresser or superficial or somethin'.

So then what happens? Well, maybe he loses confidence. *What's the point,* he might think, *she's obviously just nodding along but doesn't care. She's stroking her hair and just being nice by staying in the conversation.* Other than that, the male concludes, she's clearly not interested.

Okay. Now let's look at this scene through the lens of *un*intended messages. Let's say the woman is still stroking her hair, but she is doing it unconsciously. Sure, she's attracted to the guy, but she doesn't want that known. At least not yet. Maybe she's a little timid or soft-spoken. Maybe she's not used to being flirtatious. Whatever the reason, she doesn't intend for the guy to easily pick up on her attraction. At least not this early in the conversation.

Okay, so if the male does not receive the message—no harm no foul. She didn't want him to know anyway, and he doesn't. Now let's say he *does* receive the message. He picks up on the subconscious cue. Maybe he doesn't now it's subconscious, maybe he think she's consciously aware of her hair-stroking because she wants to make it obvious. Regardless, he sees the stroking as indicating attraction, and he makes his move from there.

The female might be taken aback if he asserts his masculinity or she might be pleasantly surprised. Whatever her reaction, she didn't expect him to know she was attracted. A number of unintended outcomes can occur.

Finally, let's say the unintended message is *mis*interpreted. In this final case, the male could think any number of things. Perhaps he thinks she has something in her hair. Maybe he thinks she's bored. Maybe he's really intoxicated and thinks she wants to jump his bones right then and there. Whatever his reaction, it is not an appropriate reaction to the signal of attraction, unintended or not.

But that's how these things work. That's how they go. It's never perfect, and sometimes messy (especially with alcohol involved!). There are many ways that body language communication is transmitted. And when it comes to the previous scenario, those many ways become even crazier.

Then again, who can be surprised? Men and women are complicated. Male and female interactions are varied. And psychosexual signaling is a complex, yet very subconscious, process. All of these things, and many more, are formulated through what we say, and what we don't. All of them, undeniably, are transmitted through the six message types.

Good.

So now that we've covered the body language message *types*, let's cover the body language message *forms*. Just to clarify, message *type* refers to the relationship between the message sender and receiver. Message *form*, by contrast, refers to the relationship between the message channel and usage. More precisely, the channel is the way the message is conveyed. And the usage is the way the message is employed to transmit its contents.

Confused?

Let's break it down further:

Kinesthetics – This *form* of body language communication is the most easily observed. It refers specifically to those actions and messages displayed and sent by the body. These of course include everything from the movement, posture and lean of the body, to the expressions of the body and face. If you smile, laugh, grimace and so on, you are sending messages in the form of kinesthetics. This form of body language communication also includes the eyes. The way you look and gaze, your blink rate, your eye movement, and the changes in your pupil size—all of these things are also included under the form of kinesthetics.

Aesthetics – This *form* of body language communication refers to the way you display yourself. Now, do not confuse this with kinesthetics. Unlike *kin*esthetics, *a*esthetics refers to the artistic. It is the message, or set of messages, you send through your clothing. Through your accessories, through your hairstyle and your makeup and your general hygiene. Aesthetics refers to how you present yourself through all of the 'things' you add to your natural body. Wearing one shirt over another, exposing some belly in one instance, while hiding your body in another—all of these factors are crucial to communicating a body language message in the form of aesthetics. And aesthetics differ depending on the receiver of the message. To one person, a guy with a ripped shirt and long hair is a loser and a degenerate. To another person, that same guy is simply 'chill.'

Linguistics – This *form* of body language communication refers to the way we talk. Not what we say when we talk, but the way we say it. Simply think of all the different people in your life. There are people who talk slow, people who talk fast, people who mumble and talk too loudly, people with accents and odd pauses, people who ramble and people who get to the point. These shifts in voice volume, pitch, intonation, frequency and deliverance are critical. Saying, *"You're great"* means one thing. But saying, *"You're… great,"* can mean something entirely different. As they say, it's not about what you say. It's how you say it.

Physicality – This *form* of body language communication refers to both physical contact and physical use of the environment. In other words, how you touch and how you space yourself. Think about your daily interactions with people. Depending upon the setting, the time and the relationship, you send different physicality messages all the time. Chances are, you'll stand closer to a family member, and be more likely to touch. But if you're passing a stranger at the supermarket, you're probably going to give more space and not initiate physical contact.

Your body language message also depends upon the fixed space you occupy. For instance, your message will differ sitting behind the wheel of a car talking to somebody outside, than it would if you were sitting in a chair talking to somebody adjacent to you. Setting and contact matter. You wouldn't pet, slap, caress or tap a total stranger, but you might your sibling. You wouldn't yell to somebody you recognize in a movie theater, but you might walking on the street.

Spatial-Temporal – This *form* of body language communication refers to when and where you are. In other words, what are your habits? If you're a person who routinely shows up early, you send a consistent message. If you are a person who routinely shows up late, you send a message. If you are a person who responds in socially acceptable ways to environmental cues (light, noise, décor, etc.), you are sending one message. If you are a person, regardless of environment, who acts in socially unacceptable ways, you are sending another message.

These body language messages are highly dependent upon the way you perceive yourself in time and place, and the way you communicate that perception. Some people can be like chameleons, adapting effortlessly to various places at various points. Other people will be like rocks, remaining the same no matter what happens. All of these factors, taken individually and together, represent a communication of significance.

But why do people do these things? Why use one form over another? Why use multiple forms when one will do? Why use only one when many are better? How do people decide how to communicate their innermost feelings and desires? Is it largely unconscious? Is it usually conscious? And ultimately, what is the reason for doing it?

Truth be told, there are multiple reasons. Here they are:

Interpersonal – You know what this means. It means how you relate to others. The way you talk to others, behave around others, feel and think about others, and physically interact with others. Body language messages are key to communicating interpersonal truths and realities. Simply think about most of your relationships. You likely have relations with all sorts of people. Some people are your friends, maybe your best friends. Others are more distant friends. Some people are mere acquaintances. Some people are just coworkers. And sometimes you come across people you may only see from time to time, if never again. These include people at the grocery store, people at movie theatres, malls, ball games, restaurants and bars, walking about and in passing.

Now think about how you use body language to relate to these people. What is the interpersonal dynamic? Do you stand close or far? Do you adorn yourself with certain accessories (shoes, watches, hats and jewelry) when in the presence of certain people but not in the presence of others? Do you seek to establish the parameters of a relationship through what you wear and say? Think about at work. You might dress differently, talk differently, use different mannerisms. You might 'hide' your true nature or intentions. Now think about being around others. Think about daughters and sons. Typically, a young woman will not wear racy clothing around her father. Now, around a hot new date…

Consider the way people move and act and send their body language messages depending upon the relationship. A kiss to the cheek of an elderly relative will mean something different than a kiss to the cheek of someone with whom you are romantic. Similarly, placing your hand on the back of that elderly relative might signal support and gratitude, but may signal to a partner sexual attraction and longing.

Bottom line is, body language messages will differ depending upon the relationship. Even if you display similar body language behaviors, they might mean entirely different things. And in some cases, displaying totally different behaviors might mean virtually the *same* thing.

Emotional Resonance – Similar to signaling a relationship, we also tend to express and manage our emotional states with body language. This body language messaging typically involves kinesthetics. You use your body to signal that you're happy. That you are mad or elated. You may smile, laugh, grin, frown, or rub your head. You may display complex emotions such as jealousy or disappointment. You may keep your body language open, extending hugs and touches, or you may be closed off, with your arms folded and your body turned. Emotional resonance is not only used to communicate how you feel about someone (looking down your nose in contempt), but how you want someone to feel about *you*.

Think of dancing and figure skating, for instance. A lot of emotive movements and expressive poses and postures. These movements are designed to elicit certain feelings and thought patterns. They are used to elicit important understandings of the world. They are used to signal universal and individual states of emotion.

Emotional resonance also features a level of deception. You feign happiness when you are sad. You show a smile, trying to hold your head high.

Or maybe you're playing poker, keeping your face emotionless, hiding your tics and keeping your arms and legs and hands steady. You keep your head straight. Maybe you pretend to be relaxed when you're nervous as hell. Whatever the reason, emotional resonance is about signaling, and eliciting, given emotions. You can essentially achieve three things with the body language messages you send: (1) communicate your own emotional state, (2) transpose your emotions onto others, and (3) create new emotions in others.

With time and skill, you can become a veritable master of emotional exploitation. A level of deceit and deception, evasion and lying, may become necessary at times. However, it is cautioned that you exercise extreme judgment when considering these maneuvers. Remember, to exploit one's emotions is to violate a basic tenet of human interactions. It is better to be honest about your feelings, to air your grievances and allow for natural healing.

Of course, sometimes we simply have to overcome, or defeat, bad situations and bad people. It's simply inevitable. This is where emotional manipulation becomes useful.

Snap Judgments – You've probably heard it before. In mere seconds after meeting you, people decide if they like you or not. They decide how they feel about you as a person, what they think about your character, your quality as a human, if you're likely to be good or bad—who you are and what you're about, even if they're totally wrong.

This is why body language is so important. Some people, unfortunately, send negative messages without even knowing it. Other people always seem to give off the right 'vibes.' But more often than not, life is about snap judgments. The way you stand and talk. If you move fluidly or seem clunky and odd. If you can command a room or control your emotions or speak with power and precision, with ease and confidence. If you are easy-going. If you stand rigid and uneasy. If you wear clothes that communicate strength or weakness. If you seem open or closed-off, if you seem like a nice person or have a resting face that is always scowling—so on and so forth.

Point is, snap judgments are critical. The body language messages we send in the opening seconds are indispensable to showing how we feel and act. This is important because it is the first impression we make on people. Whether interacting with strangers, friends, or our closest soulmates, it is important to understand why these things matter. Everything you do, subconsciously and consciously, communicates something. Sometimes, you have to make sure that *something* is what you want it to be.

Good. So now we've covered a number of highly relevant concepts and constructs related to the use of body language messaging, and more broadly, nonverbal communications. These concepts and constructs are useful because they allow us to navigate our personal and interpersonal worlds with greater ease. However, they are only concepts. They are only constructs. While they may make sense in theory, in practice, sometimes they fail. Sometimes, the world we devise in our mind is totally different from the world we discover outside it.

This is why it's important to understand what specific movements mean. What specific gestures mean. What expressions, and postures, and poses, and bodily contortions mean. It's time to get into the specifics and leave the theory behind.

It's time, to enter The Real World...

Seeing is Believing – How to Pinpoint The Top 14 Body Language Profiles

The Real World is never easy.

When you're out and about, doing your daily deeds or simply enjoying some leisure time-off, you notice things. Not only your own problems, with the usual things, but other people's problems. Other people's behaviors. Other people's attitudes and emotions and changing, strange, sometimes unpredictable moods and feelings. You notice discrepancies between thought and action, feeling and doing—you notice things. And when you notice things, you begin to realize… body language is *every*thing.

What someone says can sometimes be almost meaningless. You have to know what somebody *doesn't* say. What they do or signal. The unspoken message sent and received.

But what if you don't receive it?

What if there aren't enough messages? What if you simply can't make sense of a person given the limited information available?

This is why *profiles* are so important. As you've probably already learned, *profiles* refer to sets of body language that, taken together, communicate a general or specific message. You can't simply look at somebody's facial expression and conclude one thing. You can't simply observe a person's posture, or movement, and come to an accurate conclusion. Sure, maybe sometimes you'll get lucky. But most times, you have to dig deeper.

So without further ado, let's do just that. Let us analyze the many and various profiles of body language communication:

Antagonistic – This profile refers to messages that make you back down or back away. Fight or flight is a human defense mechanism. Some people run away from danger, some people go at it. When a person is displaying the antagonistic body language profile, he or she is going *at* it.

We can typically tell when this profile is being displayed. First, consider the face of the person nearby. When antagonistic body language begins, it is usually first observed in the face. The jaw muscles will tense, the eyes will either narrow or become intense, leading to a prolonged stare or glare. The face is generally taut with a frown or sneer or even grinding of the teeth. This all traces back to our animalistic roots, in which tensing the body is a precursor to combat.

The rest of the body is even easier to discern. The biceps may flex and the fists will clench. As blood rushes to the face, the face reddens, and the attack is prepared. You may also notice a scrunching of the eyebrows, wrinkling of the forehead, and even a baring of the teeth.

However, sometimes antagonistic body language is counter-intuitive. Not all people who are feeling aggressive will outwardly show it. Some people may actually appear more relaxed when feeling aggression. They may open their stance, showing their chest, leaning back, or even turning away, to taunt you into an attack.

It's also important to notice the space. See, we all have personal space. We have boundaries. We have areas around our bodies and things where we don't want certain people. When a person is antagonistic, he or she will purposely invade these boundaries. Sometimes, however, this 'invasion' comes under a guise. You may notice how females, especially, act as friends, entering certain areas, or violating certain boundaries, while pretending to be nice and welcoming.

Men do this too, usually with subtle bumps and nudges, while pretending to be 'okay' on the surface. Oftentimes, awkward laughter, fake smiles, and uncomfortable exchanges may ensue. When the 'invader' is not fended off, he or she has successfully exerted dominance.

Once the boundaries have been permeated, the antagonist may offer several forms of touching. Even if these forms of touching are soft and would otherwise be harmless, given the context of the permeation, they are now threatening. Furthermore, any gestures performed within this violated space are also deemed threatening. Even outside the permeation zone, many gestures clearly signal antagonism. These typically include pointing, thrusting and tilting of the chin.

Another style of antagonistic body language arrives in the form of displacement. Broadly, displacement denotes aggressive attacks on things other than the object of the aggression. In this case, the object would be the person. So instead of attacking the person, the antagonist might flip a chair or slam a table or punch a wall or lash out at some piece of furniture. Basically, the message communicated is: *this could be you.*

Sometimes, the antagonist doesn't even physically touch something. He or she may simply make an abrupt movement. Examples include jumping off from a sitting position, lunging at someone, or stomping your foot. This sudden 'pre-attack' is used to prime the individual for a potential attack, and to gauge the reaction of the other individual.

Wide-ranging gestures or movements may also signal this style of antagonism. For instance, an antagonist may throw his or her hands about the air, may sweep the air, may move about with large steps, or may thrash an invisible foe. These pronounced movements signal both a displacement of anger and hostility, and an indicator of what's yet to come.

<u>Assertive</u> – This profile of body language messages refers to a style that is calm, cool, and collected. The main takeaway from this profile is evenness. There is an evenness in one's movements, postures, poses and signals. This evenness

creates a body that is neither too loose nor too rigid. Sometimes, people seem unnaturally rigid or unnaturally loose, perhaps from drugs or fatigue. But with the assertive profile, there is a steadiness to pace and action. There is balance.

This smoothness also carries over into the voice. There are no herky-jerky words or sudden changes in pitch and tone. The talking frequency is consistent, the volume changes appropriately, and spoken words generally match the look on the face and lips. Again, evenness. Things are even, there are no contradictions or discrepancies between what is said, how it is said, and how the body is operating.

Moreover, the assertive profile signals control. The person navigates his or her environment with a steady pace and eye. He or she does not stare or dart the eyes, nor squint or widen them. The chin is kept level and the eyes look ahead.

In terms of posture, the assertive profile conveys relaxation and equity. The person is not disproportionately favoring one side. There is no noticeable slumping or depending upon objects to sit or stand a certain way. The individual is upright, the body is firm, and appendages are used equitably. Feet are typically evenly spaced.

Just imagine a balanced weight trainer at the gym. Somebody who targets all muscle groups, who is well-defined throughout. Now imagine somebody who focuses solely on one group, a 'meathead' who may have massive triceps and biceps that look odd when compared to the rest of the body. The assertive individual is the one with the balanced musculature.

When signaling through hand gestures or the use of props, the movements are proportionate. In other words, what they say matches what they do. For instance, the assertive individual isn't going to say something mundane, and then act all theatrical. Instead, exaggerations are minimized and most gestures are used functionally to highlight certain elements of what is communicated. The palms are usually visible, and the arms are kept to the sides when not gesturing.

Similarly, physical contact is neither strong nor weak. It is done sparingly but firmly, without unnecessary escalations of emotion. By and large, the face denotes gentleness and steadfastness. Even in trying situations, the face rarely signals fear or aggression.

Overall, the assertive individual exists in real-time, indicating attention, interest, and responsiveness. Warm smiles are used, as is steady contact, to create connection where necessary. Light touching, handshakes and gentle clasps help to further this connection. The assertive profile signals that the individual is ready to help, and able to do so, given situational demands.

Enthrallment – This profile refers to attention. But attention is about more than mere listening. We can listen all we want, but that doesn't mean we hear. Listening in this sense refers to the full focus of one's sensory faculties, and cognitive capacities, on the *object of enthrallment* (ie; the interesting individual)

The enthrallment profile is most notable for its ability to filter extraneous stimuli. This deep interest is displayed by a preternatural stillness in the person's body and face. Not only are they solely focused on what is going on, but even their internal thoughts are filtered to allow such focus.

Typically this individual is leaning *toward* the object of enthrallment. The head will tilt toward the source of interest, or to the side, to signal consideration of what is being said. The exposure of the neck and wrists also signifies comfort and ease. Because the listener is so intently interested, he or she does not feel threatened.

The eyes do not blink (often), and the eyebrows furrow readily. There are no interruptions, and the body language remains open. The arms may dangle loosely, the legs remain opened, and the head typically nods to signal understanding, and to urge the speaker to continue. The slower the nod, the more likely the listener understands and approves. A quicker nod may simply be a cue to *'keep going keep going.'*

Typically, the listener will also show mirroring body language. In other words, if the speaker is sitting a certain way, the listener may do the same. This mirroring establishes rapport and connection, showing that both listener and speaker are on the same wavelength. Overall, the enthrallment profile shows deep, consistent interest through calm, open body language; soft and steady vocalizations; and steady, encouraging eye contact and expressions. Typically, body contact will be used sparingly, as this may disrupt the connection between message sender and receiver.

Uninterested – It is one thing to be *dis*interested. This means we're impartial and choose not to take a stance on an issue. But it's another thing to be *un*interested, in which you specifically reject or do not care for a certain person, place or thing. This is true boredom, the absolute lack of any and all interest or inclination.

The body language of the uninterested individual is often easy to spot. Because they have literally no real interest in what is happening, they will distract themselves. Their eyes will be anywhere else, their hands and feet and arms and legs will engage in monotonous, distracting activities. They may tap their toes or roll pencils or play with their phone or watch, or watch the clock.

This repetition both signals the boredom as well as initiates an involving activity. There is also a degree of fatigue involved. The individual may further signal the lack of interest by slouching, stretching, yawning, rubbing the eyes, staring blank-eyed, rubbing the face, sighing and so on.

However, some people will actually fake a lack of interest. They may want you to think they are unprepared or uncaring. They may want to catch you off guard. If a person is faking the uninterested profile, keep a careful eye on their face. Notice their eyes. Are they alert or weary? Are their lips pursed? Are their limbs or torso rigid? Are they bobbing their legs not out of boredom but of readiness?

Be wary of people who pretend to be weary. It's an especially common tactic in sports, where athletes attempt to lull their competition into a false sense of security. They pretend to be tired or uncaring, and then they explode for a great basketball layup, or a touchdown, or a kick on goal, or a hockey shot. It happens all the time, and it certainly happens outside of sports. People use a fake uncaring attitude to convince others that they're not a threat. Remember: some people advertise their adversity. Others, let it slip in through the back door…

Shut Down – This profile refers to body language that is mostly closed off and shut down. That is to say, it is closed off to whatever stimuli is coming in. People have a lot of reasons for being closed off. They don't like somebody. They are tired. They are unsure. They are scared. They are simply not in the mood to deal with x, y, z. Whatever the reasons, the Shut Down profile indicates a disinclination, or inability, for being receptive.

You will notice this profile in a variety of ways. Firstly, people use their limbs as a sort of cocoon. Sometimes the limbs are merely touching or slightly curled, other times an individual might literally assume the fetal position.

The arms will often cross the central dividing line down the middle of the body. Fingers may clasp or hold. The evolutionary reason for this is simple. It's a protective nurturing mechanism. You are shielding yourself from incoming. You are soothing yourself by pulling away. Just like you curl up in bed at night to get comfortable and warm, the Shut Down profile curls up to find a safer space. It is pulling away from the worries and stressors of the world.

Of course, not all people are totally Shut Down mode. Some will display a path toward that body language. They may close off other vulnerable spots, like wrists and ankle and neck. They may lightly cross their limbs, or hold their hands near their face. They will likely hold tension in their face, arms, shoulders and hands.

Another thing they do is to cross the legs. There are many ways to cross the legs, whether it be at the thighs, mid-leg, ankles and so on. The person may also wrap their legs around other things, such as objects on the floor, chair legs and the like.

Notice that the head and eyes are usually lowered. This defensive lowering is usually a type of tucking, which shields the body and mind from incoming stimuli. But sometimes it's as simple as the person being tired or looking down at something.

Truth be told, there are many reasons for the Shut Down profile. Some people aren't, in fact, shutting down. They might just be cold, and so they're tightening their body for warmth. Sometimes, we simply do it for defending purposes. We makes ourselves smaller and reduce the likelihood of either being targeted or attacked. We cover the crucial areas, like the veins at the wrist and the jugular at the neck. We close off our inner thighs. We keep our chest turned or covered. We tense our muscles.

Sometimes, it's not defense but self-love. Or nurturing. Or mollycoddling. Thus, this 'hugging' of the self imitates the hugging by a parent, guardian, caretaker and/or loved one. We must also admit that such body language may simply mean the individual is taking it easy. Some of us have long limbs and just need to fold them, or cross them, to feel comfortable.

Also be mindful of persuasion. The transitions between Shut Down profiles and more open body language profiles may signify psycho-physical persuasion tactics. An individual will typically cross, then open, then recross, the arms or legs to give somebody else a certain impression. This impression may be, *"I'm listening, but not convinced, I'm listening but not convinced… yet."* Sometimes the changes in body language also signify that the individual is trying to influence you. They want you to do what they do. They want you to mirror them.

This is a common sales tactic, used to get people to come to your side without them even realizing it. If done naturally and steadily, the other person may begin to display the same movements. They will cross and uncross their legs, they will hold their hands, and they will subconsciously feel an affinity toward you. Sometimes, alternating between closed and open body language is necessary to keep people guessing. Moreover, crossing your arms across your chest may force others to work harder to persuade you. Or they might simply give up and submit.

<u>Self-Belief</u> – Confidence is often the gateway to many successes in life. If you are confident you can go and do things that others can't. Your thoughts turn to action. Your feelings are stable and strong. Your life is continuing in an upward trajectory. You know what you want and you go after it. You capitalize on confidence hacks with ease and regularity. By most accounts, you feel (and do) well. You are *constant*.

Now, when Self-Belief is constant in body language, it is constant in many ways. People that are not confident are uneasy. They dart about, they sway, they hold themselves, they look around, and they generally seem ready to be somewhere else, doing something else, acting somehow differently. They are tense and jumpy and anxious all at once. They tap their feet, they pace around. They are not balanced, they are not at ease.

If they aren't moving frantically, they're caught in molasses. They slump, they look down. They don't make eye contact, they don't make promises. They avoid conflict, and fear obstacles. They simply want *no* part of any real challenge.

But confident people on the other hand…

People displaying the Self Belief profile will stand firmly with feet placed evenly apart. They will sit evenly, back in the seat comfortably, without unnecessary leaning or slouching. Their chests will be out, their posture erect, their hands either steeples or relaxed at their sides. The body is still, the head barely moves, and a general low level of threat-anxiety is observed.

Many confident people don't want to seem exaggerated. They will not wave their arms, they will not let you know that there is reason to be alarmed. They will typically sit there and do what they want, without worry. Many times, they will clasp their hands behind the back. There is no twitching or fidgeting, and tics are minimized.

You will also notice a generally slower pace. It's measured, it has nuance. If this individual is working through a crowd, he or she will gently nudge or touch the shoulders of passing people, to cordially create space. The individual of confidence will speak easily, assuredly, without unnecessary pauses. Silence may be used confidently to create new impulses and ideas.

There are many reasons you will notice a confident person. He or she is insistent upon being forward. They face forward, they think forward, they move forward. They face people they are talking to, they shake hands firmly, they listen carefully, they act and regard others with casual respect. They generally seem like good people. They don't avoid contact, they don't avoid sharing a smile—they don't avoid, period. They approach. With power. With pride. With purpose.

A person displaying the Self-Belief profile will not back away. They will not scan for threats. They will search for friends. They look. They don't shy away. They look eye-to-eye and they don't back down from a challenge. They gesture smoothly, and they answer succinctly.

No hesitance. No awkward pausing. No fear. A confident person will not be dissuaded by fear. When something does happen, they can assess the situation with accuracy. They are not scared, they are ready. They are not discouraged, they are engaged. Remember, confidence is not arrogance. A confident person is ready to approach new obstacles with courage and conviction. They do so silently, not braggadociously. They are quietly prepared, and will not grandstand or boast of their powers without proportionate evidence. In men, they are the <u>consummate alpha male</u>. In women, they garner the respect of *all* males around.

The Self-Belief profile indicates that an individual is capable, confident, and consistent. Life may get rocky, but the body language of the Self Belief profile is stillness in a storm. They will weather the rough winds and tough.. it… out. It's incredible and it's admirable. And if somebody is a full-fledged Self-Belief profile, it's almost unstoppable.

<u>Subterfuge</u> – When one is using subterfuge, deception or deceit, one is essentially trying to avoid truthfulness. The main thing to remember in all of this is that the Subterfuge Profile requires avoidance behaviors. People who are dishonest do not want to be found out. Although some people can flawlessly lie without obvious tics or indications, most people are not so skilled. The average Subterfuge

Profile will indicate somatic reactions such as sweating, jerkiness, tension and twitching, and sporadic shifts in the tone, speed or frequency of spoken words.

Be mindful, the Subterfuge Profile will seek to hide tells. The individual may wrap his arms behind his back, hide bobbing legs beneath a desk, hide hands in pockets, touch or rub or attempt to casually caress his or her body. This is done in an attempt to naturalize physical manifestations of anxiety.

Think about it. If you're super nervous about being exposed, you might try to hide your anxiety. Instead of jumping all around, you will reroute your physical oddities in a way that is plausible. You might pretend to stretch, pretend you have an itch, pretend you are adjusting your clothing—anything to channel your physical nerves in a way that is less obvious.

Some people will truly internalize their nerves to an extent that is hard to detect. They might subtly grind their teeth, bite their lips, squeeze their fists, or tense parts of their body that are not visible. And be mindful, not all anxious behaviors indicate deception. Plenty of people get anxious and nervous for other reasons. So look further...

The Subterfuge Profile will also typically overcompensate to hide deception. People who are deceiving will constantly try to over-control their attitudes and behaviors. They will force smiles (which do not touch the eyes), they will try to stand very still to hide anxiousness, and they will often look you directly in the eyes (to an uncomfortable point). These tactics are used to keep us thinking they are honest. The deceiver will also try to find a balance between the Shut Down Profile and more opened body language. They do this because they believe that these shifts are natural—and they are.

But not when enacted by the deceiver.

The deceiver will incorrectly, ineffectively, sporadically shift between various Profiles, thinking that this demonstrates normal human behavior. But to the keen observer, these unpredictable, unnecessary changes are only a greater admission of guilt.

The Subterfuge Profile also often struggles to keep pace. Because the individual is internally obsessed with hiding the truth and perpetuating the lie, he or she may seem out-ofsync. He or she may not react accordingly to certain events or news, instead acting too calculated. This lack of natural human reactions can be a dead giveaway. Say, for instance, a person is guilty of attacking someone else.

And you say, *"Did you hear John got beat up the other night?"* And the person, in an attempt to disguise his guilt, says *"Oh... oh, I... no, no I didn't..."* Responses may be measured or ill-timed. They may simply lack a sense of normalcy. Oftentimes, we have an intuitive feeling about liars without quite knowing why. This is one of those cases.

Now let's assume that the Subterfuge Profile is not nefarious. Sure, an individual may use deception and deceit and half-lies and white lies, but what if it's for 'good' reasons?

There are many reasons we don't tell the complete truth. We do so to avoid tough situations. To protect others from damaging information. To protect ourselves. To preserve what we deem to be the greater good. We do a lot of things and say a lot of things for a lot of reasons. When it comes to 'lying' sometimes so-called 'lying' is better than telling the truth.

It all depends on the eye of the beholder…

Trusting – this Profile is concerned with one thing and one thing only: communicating and gaining trust. The easiest thing to notice is the open body language. Vulnerable spots on the body are exposed, such as the wrists and inner legs. The posture is open, and no physical barriers are in the way. People positioned behind chairs or tables, or using props for support, are less trustworthy. They are hiding something. They are protecting themselves from something. Trustworthy people, by contrast, do not hide themselves, do not protect themselves, and do not use bodily movements such as crossing their arms or legs, to close down. They are not trying to conceal anxiety, frustration or tension.

Noticing the facial expressions is important too. Somebody you can trust, who is willing to trust you, is apparently relaxed. The individual may nod and keep the head and eyes on even keel with yours. They are steady in their movements, their speech, their gaze, their head motions, their gestures—everything. The don't come close, unless touching to show understanding or concern or empathy. Otherwise, they stand at least a few feet away, but close enough for you to see their pupils. They will nod when they disagree, purse their lips during periods of emotion, furrow their brows in concern, tilt their body just slightly, and turn their head just a tad when measuring your words.

Overall, the Trusting Profile is ready to listen and help, if needed. The individual wants to improve your life. The individual wants to change your life. The individual wants you to feel that you can do the same. But more than anything, the individual wants you to trust that it can happen.

Domineering – This Profile references that oh-so-lovely human tendency to dominate. Some people dominate because they embody dark psychopathy. Others dominate simply because, well, they like feeling like the powerful one. Whatever the reasons, the Profile is often easy to spot.

First, look for the stance or posture of the Domineering. There are three things they will do to increase domination. They will increase their size, their height, and their presence. This means that the individual will try to appear bigger than they are. This can be achieved by stretching their arms wide, by standing abnormally erect with a thrusted chest and by placing their legs far apart while sitting or standing.

Also notice the way the person physically contacts you. Many times, they will initiate contact. This is done, simply, so that *you* have to react to *them*.

In greeting, he or she more likely than not will use a handshake, firm, over-the-top, palm-down. The Domineering may squeeze tightly to show dominance. In order to counter, grab them by the elbow, immediately return any physical contact, and/or step to the side to catch them off guard.

The individual will also seek to stand high. If the individual is naturally shorter than you, notice how he or she acts. Does the individual stand on a higher platform? Do they offer a chair that is lowered? Do they wear platforms? Do you force you to crouch or lower yourself in some way? Do they stand on a step? This difference communicates not only that they are physically bigger, but that they are figuratively 'larger' and thus more significant.

The Domineering Profile also likes to occupy space. This consumption of available space indicates an ability to consume resources, to assert territory, and to minimize threats posed by intruders. The Domineering Profile may also encroach upon your own space, as if to say, *'All of this is mine.'* Whilst in these spaces, the Domineering Profile will also bend or break social etiquette. They may wear what they please, say what they please, and boss others around.

Oftentimes, signals of power correlate with wealth. The Domineering Profile will remind you of their power by discerning objects or items of value, often flaunting them or using them casually, as if to say, *'this is nothing to me.'*

Also, be mindful of positioning. The Domineering Profile loves to sit in positions that demonstrate power, wealth and discernment. They will sit at the head of a big table, stand at the center of a room, in the middle of a route, forcing others to move, forcing others to stand around them. Why? Because this is gravitas. They act as if they are their own gravitational body, and others must revolve around them. They are the epicenter, the cohesion, the centerfold, the superior.

They will dominate all aspects of a room or space. They will exploit their own and others' furniture and accouterments. They will casually use what they want, as they want. It may come across as pompous or confident, but in reality it is meant to show dominance.

It communicates, *'I do what I want, and there's nothing you can do about it.'*

When noting the Domineering Profile, look for facial expressions: pursed lips, scowls, frowns, slight frowns—all of these expressions indicate an appraisal of personal power and control.

Note the situation. The Domineering Profile will display smugness and contempt in situations where they should be humble. The eyes may look away, not out of fear or avoidance, but as if to say, *'you're irrelevant.'* The eyes may also squint, as an intimidation tactic or to hide where they are actually looking. The face is usually kept relaxed, casual, inexpressive. This is done because it communicates, *'You are not a threat, I am the superior.'*

Men and women will also make figurative displays of the genitals. For men, it signals physical endowment or more broadly, confidence. For women, it signals a comfort in body and mind. Although some women may fear that such openness is an advertisement to leering males, the Domineering Profile fears not. She will openly show her physical attributes, confident in her power to deflect unwanted attention.

If you find yourself encountering somebody who is domineering, don't be intimidated. Tell them how you feel, or better yet, show them. Squeeze firmly on the handshake. Stare at their nose, so that you are not the one breaking eye contact first. Be cool, be normal. If need be, ignore the signals. Act like nothing is out of the ordinary. Be confident, be careful, but most importantly, be proactive. Don't wait for them to dictate how you behave. Talk first, act first. And whenever the opportunity arrives, call the individual out on his or her obvious attempt to dominate. Nothing undermines the Domineering Profile like a well-timed, keen and witty remark.

Examiner – This Profile does exactly what it says. It examines. It questions. It observes and analyzes and judges and assesses. It takes the distinct and interrelated attitudes and behaviors of a given individual, and makes sense of them. When the Examiner Profile is in action, it will typically display a number of body language signals. Firstly, it clasps its hands together in a pensive, evaluative manner. This may mean steepling of the hands, tapping of the fingers, or a triangular pressing of the fingertips together. The fingers may rest at the abdomen, between the legs, or even at the lips.

Notice the eyes. Dilated pupils indicate increased brain activity, and the touching or caressing of the face in a pondering fashion indicates an ongoing thought process. Also, be mindful of the head position. Some people may be resting their chin in their hands as their eyebrows furrow, their forehead scrunches, and their thoughts continue. The body is typically relaxed, as the head (brain) is the most active.

The important thing to remember about the Examiner Profile is the focus on truth and facts. The Examiner is seeking to uncover the truth and sift through the lies. A focused, calm, cool demeanor is indicative of this inclination.

<u>Receptive</u>- This Profile refers to those who are willing to receive. They receive messages, threats, emotions, thoughts, behaviors, whatever. They are generally open to the

messages you send, and are capable of receiving them accurately at the highest rate of any Profile.

Receptive body language is easy to see. The wrists are exposed, the neck is exposed, the eyes are open and watching, the eyebrows are raised in curiosity, the body is engaged with information, nodding as information is digested, arms bobbing as excitatory impulses increase, and the general posture of the body forward and focused.

The eyes are focused in a natural way, and the environment is noted but not distracting. The Receptive Profile fancies stimulating engagement, whether mental, emotional or physical. The Receptive Profile wants to think, feel and do, and will seek individuals who consistently enable this. Active body language messages are preferred over passive ones.

However, the Receptive Profile can, itself, be very passive. Although not to the point of submissive, the Receptive Profile will readily expose vulnerable physical spots of the human body, including the inner arms, legs, and crotch. Women may feel confident in exposing greater extents of their feminine bodies. This level of exposure signals both relaxation and passivity. The passivity comes from a conscious or subconscious need to be guided. The Receptive Profile shows the body, as if to say *'this is me, I come in peace'* and to avoid being potentially accused of hiding. The Receptive Profile is often more easily swayed than others, and constantly seeks an 'alpha' leader to take the reins.

<u>Sexual</u> – This Profile, as is obvious, refers to body language that is sexual in nature. It is body language that people like to see, experience, and ultimately understand. It is the type of body language that can maximize sexual potency and improve relationship intimacy for a long, long time. This is very important for a number of reasons:

The Sexual Profile is the key to a night of fun love, or to a night spent alone… Okay, okay, maybe not always, but in many cases—yes. By sending the right sexual signals and communicating the appropriate level of sexual interest, we can succeed beyond our wildest dreams.

Initially, look for mirroring. The Sexual Profile will mimic body language in order to show liking and reciprocity. Remember, imitation is the highest form of flattery. Next, seek the face. Notice if the eyes hold contact for longer than usual, than divert. This is often easiest to notice in a crowded room, where a keen prolonged gaze can be traced to somebody across the room. It may be difficult to know if that gaze is for you, so return the look, hold eye contact, and if the individual breaks, flushes, or breaks and looks back—you've got yourself a person of interest…

Self-fashioning is also critical. The Sexual Profile will increase that sexual profile by tending to hygiene. Men may adjust their shirts to highlight their musculature. They may comb or fix their hair. They may bunch their pants in the front to accentuate the 'bulge' or to highlight strong, firm legs. The brushing off of lint, the application of cologne, and the tightening of formal attire, all signify an interest in 'looking good.'

Women are much the same. Females will often preen. They will stroke their hair, apply makeup or lipstick, rub off their clothes, adjust their clothes to highlight their attributes, rub their fingernails, hold their purses and stroke their legs.

Speaking of stroking, the Sexual Profile will also display overt actions of intent.

An action of intent is an action conducted specifically to show what is wanted or desired. For instance, a woman may stroke a phallic object or touch their lips or extend their tongue when drinking. A man, likewise, may firmly touch, bob, or even thrust inanimate objects nearby. In passing, male and females may also signal this desire by brushing up against each other.

Oftentimes, pelvic and chest contact signify a more direct intent. Women may also allow their swaying arms or hands to gently brush up against a man's body, or even crotch, in passing. These subtle but powerful indicators are clearly hinting at further contact...

There are a number of ways that the Sexual Profile can expedite the attraction/seduction process. One key psycho-sexual gambit is to elicit jealousy. Intermittent reinforcement is key.

Never give a man or woman undivided, unearned attention. Employ both interest and un-interest to keep a target of seduction on high-alert. Never serve it up on a silver platter. In order to elicit jealousy, and to prove attraction, try feigning interest in others. Talk with another man or woman, or even flirt with that man or woman, in the presence of your target. Make the target want you even more, show that you are not easily swayed, that you have to be won over, not the other way around.

Playing 'hard-to-get' can be a very effective tool. But don't ignore obvious signals. If your target makes an overt move (private touching, leaning close, whispering in your ear, groping, etc.), be sure to reciprocate. Just don't reciprocate all the way. If the target touches you lightly in a private area, return the favor but touch the target—just not as privately. Make him or her chase you, allowing him or her to escalate. This will facilitate sexual exhilaration and build until you both have reached the *tension-breaking point*.

And always, always, be confident in your assets. We can't all look like movie stars, but we can look good with what we've got. Strut your stuff, show off your figure, or your wit, or your smoothness, or your intellect, or your knowledge, or your charisma, so on and so forth. Show off and get close.

Align your body language. Show the direction of your sexual interests. Point with a finger, allow your leg and toes to point toward the target. Face with your body, with your eyes, align and lock. If you want sex, look over the body. If you want something closer to a lasting relationship, look mostly in the eyes.

The eyes are the windows to the soul.

<u>Persuasive</u> – This Profile is most frequently used in the world of commerce, business and sales. Individuals embodying these signals will typically appear to be approachable. Their body language is open, their words are inclusive and interesting, and their head and eyes show wakefulness and preparedness.

Although the Persuasive individual is assertive, he or she is not going to dominate. Domination does not require persuasion, it wins by sheer will and power. The Persuasive Profile, by contrast, wins by touching on points of import. The Profile increases relevancy with personal connections, shows control of speech, notes key points, and generally facilitates questioning and answering. This openness makes others feel comfortable and trusting.

The Persuasive Profile also capitalizes on the powers of mirroring. They will initially adopt an open and accepting stance until you too have subconsciously mimicked them. They may even initially mirror your exact body language. After the unconscious connection is cemented, the Persuasive Profile begins its own movements and moves, using gestures and expressions for all sorts of sales marketing and signaling.

The Persuasive Profile also uses posture perfectly. By casually leaning in, the Profile signals a level of submissiveness, as if to bow, but also in doing so encroaches on your personal space. This dichotomy facilitates a closeness, so that while you like the deference, you are, in fact, giving away some of your personal boundaries.

The Profile will typically persuade you in a number of ways. Firstly, alternating head positions. Nodding and tilting the head when questioning or listening. The eyebrows may raise to raise questions, and the voice may pause to signal your chance for a response. Gentle and slow breathing and nodding indicate ease and trust, while subtle expressions of pain and discomfort signal disagreement. Oftentimes the Profile will use the hands—steepled or opened with palms exposed—to indicate varying levels of interest. Steepled hands indicate thinking and feeling. Palms exposed indicate more receptivity.

In general, the Persuasive is not outright about negative emotions. While positive feelings may be displayed much more readily (smiles, laughs, friendly pats or clasps, jovial, playful jabs or gestures), negative emotions are often carefully displayed. They may be as simple as slight frowns, scrunching eyebrows, or slight shakes of the head. This encourages the target of persuasion to be reinforced by the positive and not antagonized by the negative. As the saying goes, you catch more flies with honey than vinegar.

<u>Subservient</u> – This Profile can often overlap with the Sexual Profile, but not always. In many cases, the Subservient seeks simply to show inferiority and nothing more. The submissiveness and inferiority communicate one core message: *I am beneath you.*

When showing subservience, there is a slight downward tilt of the head and body. The eyes may look to the ground more than to those around. The arms and legs may cross and the shoulders may slump. Generally, the body is closed off to decrease size and to minimize perception of threat. The Subservient signals that he or she is a willing follower. Not a leader. Not a pacesetter. The Subservient may also demonstrate fear through this closed body language, using the decreased size as a protective mechanism.

Also notice where the Subservient stands in a room relative to others. Oftentimes, behind others or to the side of others. Certainly, away from any central location. The Subservient may choose a lower footing or level if there are multiple heights. On an incline, the Subservient will stand closer to the bottom. If on even footing, or if even taller naturally, the Subservient will slump and wither to decrease size and height.

Control of movement is also critical. The Subservient will often cease to move, or at least refrain from making sudden or noticeable motions. The Subservient does not venture far, and does not want to be singled out for anything. He or she will make sure to move slowly and silently to avoid seeming aggressive or violent. The eyes might be large and fearful, or simply large and awestruck. There is smiling and there is hesitant laughter. By most accounts, the Subservient wishes only to please.

When worried, the Subservient is most noticeable. The skin becomes ashen, and the individual may shake or tremble or make erratic movements, or simply cease to move at all. He or she may speak squeamishly, softly, and generally timidly. He or she may hide behind objects or others. He or she may gesture to distant problems in subtle ways, not wanting to be noticed or targeted.

Overall, the Subservient wants to be like a fly on the wall. Noticing things, but with no responsibility in managing those things.

Okay.

Now let's take a step back. We've just deconstructed the most important body language profiles around. They are clusters of behaviors and unspoken communications that you've probably seen all over the place. However, you've likely never taken the time to break 'em down.

Which is what we just did.

But remember, just because somebody displays *behaviors* commensurate with a certain Profile, this doesn't mean the individual actually has the *feelings* associated with that Profile. And profiles can and do overlap. And interrelate. Don't forget, many people are highly deceptive. They can be sexual one moment, subservient the next, domineering after, uninterested after that, and on and on and on.

Bottom line: people change. Some do it on purpose, some accidentally. Some subconsciously. Some people are like chameleons, and some will only ever show a few Profiles. Other people may exhibit *all* Profiles, in short time. You must be aware of not only the individual, but his or her preferences, tendencies, and the current environment.

Basically, it's no easy task. Which is why an even closer look is required.

So let's take a look. Let's dive even deeper into what these individual movements, motions, and gestures really mean...

Key Gestures that Change The Game – How to Analyze & Capitalize

You can look at whatever you want.

But the longer you look at it, the longer you're resisting your natural intuitive reactions, and the longer you're *overthinking* what should be a process largely devoid of thinking.

But hey, we're people. We're humans. We have a tendency to complicate simple issues, to inject our emotions and thoughts into one another in one, big, crazy mess.

This is what happens when we observe body language. And this is why, it's important to know what we're looking at— really looking at.

Many common gestures, motions and positions signal one thing, one time, and a totally different thing another time. If you can become skilled at *consciously* recognizing the subtle differences in meaning and context, then you can slowly, but surely, become skilled at *subconsciously* recognizing those differences too.

Remember, the trick is to be natural. Body language is natural. Oftentimes, we know intuitively that someone is lying, or that someone is bad, or good, or hiding something—but we second-guess. We over-intellectualize our natural perceptions, and convince ourselves otherwise.

So let's not do that. Let's dive deeper, and explore some of the most pervasive—both powerful and subtle—body language signals out there...

(1) Feeling Fibers

We all touch our clothing from time to time. It's hot outside, we're itchy, something just bit us, we feel uncomfortable, we have a stain, we just feel the need to adjust. Many times we do it without thinking. Many times we make a conscious effort to preen and groom, to ensure that our appearance is acceptable for a given situation, setting and/or circumstance. Sometimes, we just *have* to rip off a loose thread or brush off some bothersome piece of lint.

By and large, touching our clothing is nothing odd.

However, it does signal a whole lot. These simple non-verbal touching behaviors can best be described as *redirects*.

What are we redirecting, you ask?

Well, in most cases we're redirecting an emotion, feeling, thought and/or action. Think about a time you were talking to someone. Let's say you were saying what you felt, being honest, and the person nearby was listening. Now, was the person nearby showing agreement, or disagreement?

You may have noticed the individual casually, subtly focusing elsewhere. Perhaps, the individual was checking his or her phone. Maybe the individual brushed off the pants, or rubbed the shoulder, or pretended to eye something on his shirt or jacket.

Oftentimes, these redirecting behaviors allow us to 'explain' ourselves without using words.

See, sometimes people don't want to openly disagree. They don't want to state their true opinion. Maybe they're just not in the mood, or don't care enough, or are actively trying to avoid conflict.

No matter the reason, they will often *redirect* this temptation to talk into a small physical action, such as picking at their clothes, brushing off a shoe, adjusting a collar or sleeves—or something else. Some people will make it even more obvious, using a clearing of the throat or slight cough as they redirect.

Now, sometimes this redirecting is done out of nervousness. Instead of saying something regrettable or undesired, the individual will nervously pick at his or her clothes, or scroll quickly (and sometimes pointlessly) through a phone or device.

When somebody displays these redirecting behaviors, be wary. You might think the individual is completely on-board with what you've said, but in reality he or she is likely withholding information. Furthermore, the individual may even be trying to distract *your* train of thought, through these small, but consequential actions.

You've probably noticed this before. Somebody nods or says *'definitely definitely'* even as he or she looks away, uninterested, brushing at the clothes. In other words, anything but *'definitely.'*

So be wary. Don't assume someone agrees or is even listening, just because the words say one thing. Look at the actions, look for the redirecting, and notice if the individual seems to be physically moving the hands and fingers rather than physically moving the lips in honest response. What the mouth doesn't say, the body does.

(2) The Nod

The Nod is important because the Head is important. Your head is crucial for several reasons. Firstly, it's where the brain is located. Secondly, it's where the windows to the soul—the eyes—are located. And thirdly, it's where your mouth, your speaking apparatus, is located. The head is integral because it pertains to how you think, feel and ultimately act. And even though you may keep the rest of your body still to hide your true feelings, it is the head, and your eyes, and your micro-expressions, that ultimately give you away…

Let's review some basic aspects of that head. First, and most obvious, is the nod. In many cases, the nod simply says that you agree or consent. It is essentially a submitting movement, a shortened bow, as if to say, *'I see your viewpoint and I concur.'* It is a sensory gesture, meaning that even people born without, or with diminished, sensory faculties will use the head to signal agreement.

However, the nod is not merely used to signal agreement or submission. The head nod can also be employed to convince others to do, think and feel as you wish. Take for instance, people who nod repeatedly but don't know why. The reason they are nodding may have to do with the fact that another person is nodding. Like yawning, nodding is highly contagious and will increase the likelihood of you agreeing with a nodding other, even if you don't really agree with him or her otherwise.

Studies find that nodding slowly signals interest and encourages continued talking by a speaker. Meanwhile, nodding quickly shows that enough has been said and you wish for either a turn to speak or for the speaker to change the conversation. Typically, it only takes several (three) nods at normal intervals to have the most powerful effect. So nod quickly or nod slowly, just know why you are nodding, and send a subtle signal. If you're crafty, you can steer the other person to agree with you, consent to what you're saying, change the subject, stop talking, and/or any number of things.

Interestingly, nodding creates positive feelings inside us. We unconsciously nod when we are feeling content and agreeable. And we unconsciously feel content and agreeable, simply by nodding. Just as forcing a smile will increase feelings of happiness, forcing a soft but regular head nod will increase feelings of agreeableness.

The nod can also be enhanced a number of ways. Using your finger to touch your temple or rub your chin is also critical. Used in conjunction with the head nod, this signals that you are listening and weighing the options. It is not threatening, but rather assessing and evaluating so the other person will feel comfortable.

If you would like to question someone, without coming on too strong, simply use this approach. Refrain from saying much (as your words could implant false impressions), and instead simply nod. Once the person has finished talking, explaining, and so on, give a series of 3 to 5 easy nods, and the individual will likely keep talking. This is an effective way to garner information from someone, while keeping his or her guard down, and making him or her feel as if nothing personal is being divulged.

A great tactic for a little… 'interrogating' !

(3) Chair Games

In all of the tactics of body language manipulation, few inanimate objects are more effective than the chair. The chair is the most common tool used for sitting. We spend time in chairs in cubicles, at school, in restaurants, at home, watching television, watching performances, watching seminars, watching and observing and processing a whole number of things. Bottom line: chairs are ubiquitous.

Thus, it is no surprise that body language associated with chairs is also ubiquitous. One common example of chair-body language is a maneuver called the chair-leg contortion. You've probably seen it. One person is sitting in a chair properly, with the arms on the body or armrests, and the feet either planted on the floor or reclined. Then there is another person. This person strews one leg or both legs over the arm of the chair.

This pose signals a number of things. Firstly, it communicates territory. *'This is my chair'* it says. But it also communicates dominance, indifference and even antagonistic tendencies. Sure, some people may relax with their legs over chairs, having a good time and a good conversation, maybe watching a football game or playing video games or simply chatting and cracking jokes...

But what about in other situations?

When the leg goes over the armrest, this is a signal that somebody is challenging you. They are saying *'forget etiquette, forget what you are saying.'* They might be listening to you, but they aren't engaged by it. The individual is indifferent and unmoved, doing what he or she wants, the way he or she wants to do it.

Like many body positions, this position affects the actual hormones, thought processes, feelings, emotions and behaviors of the individual. The body and mind follow a feedback loop. Your mind follows your body which follows your mind. So, if you wish to change the way you are currently feeling and thinking, change your pose.

The same can be done to someone else...

In fact, this can be done craftily a number of ways. If you wish to change somebody else's pose, and thus his or her feelings and thoughts, start by pointing or motioning. Get that other person to look at something behind them, forcing them to turn. You can even move and force them to face what you're talking about. You can also force them to catch something or grab something. Whatever you do, you must force them to change positions to change their feelings. This is critical in an argument or negotiation, where the individual will continue to softly oppose you unless the body position changes.

Of course, there are many positions to the chair. People will also use the chair like it's their own personal defense system. They may straddle it, positioning themselves and the chair so as to shield from potential attack, whether physical or psychological.

Many people engage this evolutionary response by using protective behaviors while sitting. If not turning the back of the chair for a partial blockade, they may use other objects. Such objects include obstruction via a pole, a door, a table or desk, a fence or gate, wall, a post, and any number of other fixed or movable objects and surroundings.

However, straddling a chair by itself is the most common. This body position denotes alpha status. It shows the groin, it sets the legs in firm, evenly-planted fashion. It is steadfast and sturdy, and it doesn't want to succumb to *you*.

One way to disarm this position is to change your own position. Don't mirror the straddle, but instead approach the person's exposed back. Sit or stand nearby, thus subjecting that person to potential attack. This will make the individual uncomfortable and vulnerable, and may force him to change position quickly.

You can also pre-stage the environment to discourage these sorts of behaviors. If a chair has large armrests, it will be a lot harder to straddle. Try to encourage an individual to sit in such a chair to prevent straddling in the first place.

Of course, preventing straddling is only one move in this Game of Bodies. Other individuals will relegate to the hands behind the head pose. This posturing similarly denotes domination and authority, but in a deceivingly relaxed way. It's a common pose in the world of business, in which professionals use the apparent relaxation to communicate superiority.

It says, *'I've got everything I need'* or *'I'm not intimidated by anything.'*

In this pose, the elbows stick out like sharp weapons, and the hands are hidden. The individual is ready to reveal them at any time, however. One way to deal with this position is to engage the person with an open gesture, such as wrists and palms up. You can pose a question, then see if it is answered. You can introduce a new stimuli, forcing the person to move or look or crane his or her neck. You can also try mimicking the position to signal that you are not subordinate.

In women, this position is rarely used, as it shows the breasts and may be associated with sexual interest rather than superiority. Women, however, *can* counter the position by standing up and moving, feigning disinterest as they pose questions. A subtle hand to the shoulder can also help to shift the power balance.

Generally, subordinates at work will not display this sitting position to their boss. If they do, they are often considered disrespectful. The best counter, is to move about, forcing the individual to use the arms to either signal something, or forcing the individual to change chair positions out of vulnerability.

Another chair position is the inducing of preparedness. This preparedness posturing is typically observed with several features. Firstly, it includes a forward-leaning posture. The individual will be sitting with the hands on the knees, or gripping the chair, or slightly drumming or playing on the body. Basically, the person looks ready to jump up and dart away.

Also look for nodding. The person will nod quickly, as if to say *'let's go'* and will either conclude with a *thought-gesture*, such as rubbing the chin or scratching the temples, or conclude with a *decline-gesture*, such as crossing the arms or legs.

When these behaviors are observed, it is incumbent upon you to change the game. Refocus on something different, or end the current conversation and allow an opportunity to stand up, walk around, or go to a different location.

Oftentimes, merely giving the individual a chance to move and think, can change an opinion *just* enough. Follow up with an innocuous comment, keeping your voice soft and steady. When asking a question, keep it open-ended.

If you're looking to persuade or call to action, this minor change may be all that is necessary.

(4) The Shake

This basic, evolutionary response indicates a general discontent with what is happening, or a sense of disagreement, or a direct rejection. When we're young, we shake our heads to say we don't want more food or milk from our parents. The infant shakes its head to say *'no,'* just as the rest of us shake to indicate negatives as well.

Of course, it's often way more complicated. If you shake your head to say *'no'* while your words say *'yes,'* you're in a conundrum. There are many ways that you can contradict yourself, and a well (or poorly) timed head shake makes all the difference. To keep someone guessing, shake your head when expressing agreement, and nod your head when expressing disagreement. This may totally confuse the other person, but it will also keep them engaged to try to figure you out.

And once you have another person working to figure *you* out… you've got 'em right where you want 'em!

Think of it.

If somebody is totally perplexed, interested, unsure, or caught-off-guard by you, what does that person do? What is the priority? Does that person worry more about his or her own problems, or more about you? And if that person is focused more on you, than him or herself, *you* are in control. This is a great tactic to use in heated discussions, debates, negotiations, and generally contentious discourse. Just be balanced with it. Occasionally send signals that are proportionate and expected, juxtaposed with contradictory, incongruous words, head nods and shakes.

(5) Chin Music

Another feature of the head that we use is the chin. Using your chin hinges on positioning your chin. You've probably seen it many times before. Smug, conceited, contemptuous people will look down their noses at you. They do this by tilting the head back so that the chin sticks out. This is a symbol of superiority, almost as if the chin is now a bumper, there to merely brush us mere *peasants* away...

Also notice how the vulnerable parts of the neck, the throat and jugular, are open in this position. This display of superiority communicates that they are not threatened by you, as if to say, *'go ahead, try to do something, I dare you.'*

The optics of size also important. The greater the chin juts out, the more pronounced that chin. Thus, the larger it appears. This serves a critical purpose. Larger chins are associated with superiority and alpha status, because higher testosterone often correlates with bigger chins and jaws.

Of course, not all people are using ridiculous chin displays to show superiority. Many times you will see neutral positions, which include the eye and face on even keel. In these cases, the individual may make small nods and nothing more, simply signaling for you to continue.

When the head is bowed *down*, it is usually a signal of submissiveness, deference, respect, or low self-esteem. An avoidance of eye contact may signal lack of self-esteem, but in some cases, deception. When somebody is trying to hide something, they may hide their eyes. However, in most cases a deceptive person will overcompensate by looking *too* much into your eyes.

Oftentimes, an individual is critically thinking or evaluating with the head down. The best way to change this body language and the negative perceptions that come with it, is to involve your audience. Give the person something to look at, a reason to look up, or make a sound, such as tapping a desk or noting a prop, in order to shift the focus from downward to you.

Not only will this break the downward focus, but it will actually change the emotions of your target. Research shows that simply sitting up and standing erect will increase feelings of confidence by changing your hormones. It really happens that quickly.

One final display of importance is *the tilt*. That is, the tilting of the head to the side. This is the ultimate submissive head position because it mimics infantile expressions of comfort and subordination, in which small children and animals will rest their weary heads against their parents. It also shows the neck and increases openness to threat, so it is only used when trust is given to the 'dominant' person present.

Females use this head position significantly more frequently than men. In fact, many artistic depictions and portraits and pictures and advertisements have women tilting their heads. This adds an element of submission, trust, and even seduction. The tilted head also signifies that you are being heard, your words interesting, and your words evaluated. Next time, return the favor of a slight tilt, and watch your interpersonal connections improve.

(6) The Turtle

But only if improvement is desired. Many people do not desire improvement. You may notice when certain people are afraid to show trust, afraid to show compassion, afraid to communicate any sort of ability or power. When somebody performs 'the turtle,' you will notice several things...

Firstly, you will see the head retract downward, as the shoulders go up around it. This hides the neck, throat, and even chin from attack. This is both a shrug and a duck. You are shrugging to show that you are unsure or unwilling to challenge. And you are ducking because you want to appear smaller and not cause conflict.

The Turtle is easily noticed for a number of reasons. Firstly, it signals that the individual is hiding. Secondly, it signals that the individual is not willing to engage. Thirdly, it signals that the individual deems you or those nearby as some sort of threat, whether emotional, mental, physical or spiritual. The individual may simply want nothing to do with *anybody*, or may be reacting to a question. In some cases, this duck/shrug move may follow a probing question, signaling that the individual wishes to avoid answer truthfully or fully.

(7) Springloaded

However, not all people will retreat from danger. Some are ready to sprint head-on into the flames of fury. They will enjoy the fury, relish the fury, take the fury by storm and love every minute of the fury. They will do what they want to do and do it well, do it best, on the hot coals of pressure and stress.

The human body will exhibit readiness for physical aggression a number of ways. Just think of animals. Hairy animals make their head stick out. Puffer fish will expand, birds may extend their wings, bulls and hogs may snort and huff, and all sorts of animals will boost their profile by showing their arsenal.

Humans, however, have another way. Aside from standing erect with their bodies open and ready, with their heads held high and their eyes on the prize, humans also like to use their hands. Specifically, their hands on their hips.

You've probably seen it a million times before. When waiting in the checkout line, preparing for an athletic event, during a verbal argument, in expectation of a response—no matter where you go, people put their hands on their hips. Why? Because they are waiting to handle whatever comes next. This pose makes us appear larger than we are, highlights the sharpness of elbows and half-raised hands as weapons, and generally indicates a willingness to proceed.

Of course, this pose does not necessarily mean anger or threat. The individual may simply be ready to figuratively 'attack' new challenges, such as career, academic, social, political, psychological—you name it. Many times, this hands-on-hip approach is exactly what you want to see. It means the person is forward-thinking, optimistic, hard-working, and goal-oriented.

It is also important to note other details, such as the aesthetics. An aggressive individual will have the clothing somehow opened, to expose the body. It might be a ripped or unbuttoned jacket, a shirt partially open, a coat pulled back, etc. If the clothing fully contains the body, then the individual is likely more confident than aggressive. If, however, you notice tension in the face, arms, and especially fists, you can bet that the individual is 'ready' not for chasing goals, but for starting fights.

In women, the meaning slightly differs. Typically, the hands (or one hand) on the hips signal the body. It can be to accentuate the hips and fertility, to signal sexual prowess, to highlight womanly curves, or to challenge other women to show what they have. This posture may also be used to catch men off guard, to distract them and shift the power dynamic, especially in generally male-dominated circles.

And when men or women allow their arms to dangle, or to frame, their genitals… they are clearly advertising their sexual aggressiveness! Like gorillas in the wild, some men will basically 'point' to their genitals, as if to say, *'look what I'm packin!'*

Unfortunately, this is not the best body language to use when flirting with a woman. Women want to be chased, but they don't want the chase to end quickly. If you are a guy standing there, essentially holding your junk, staring at a woman, you're being too obvious. A better approach is to not directly face her, but to force her to position herself so that she is more directly facing *you*. Turn the tables, so to speak, and become a master of the game.

Never be afraid to size up the competition. Men and women do it all the time subconsciously, even as they talk about unrelated topics. Whether doing a hands-on-the-hips, or framing their genitals, or keeping their hands in their pockets, the best way to end the tension is to stand more openly.

However, this is a strategic point. Try to notice what the individual is showing and not showing. Is the hand somewhere where it shouldn't be? Does the individual stand and allow part of the body to be covered or obscured, even when the rest of the body appears open?

This may signal a shortcoming, or insecurity, of the body. Also look for half-and-half behaviors. For instance, the individual may have one fist clenched, but is turned away, shielding the body with the other arm limp. Or, the individual may be facing you with chest and abdomen open, but hands guarding the genitals. If so, you may have just found a 'weak point' of the person in question…

But don't just question what you see. Question everything around you. When somebody is sitting a certain way, they are sitting that way for a reason. Take for instance, the distance of their leg-spread. Men will spread their legs wide to make their genital region more visible. This is a preparatory pose that signals dominance to other men. Less dominant men may close their legs or turn their bodies. Thus, the openness of the dominant man can often prevent further conflict and aggression.

There is also the effect on women. Women who see men displaying in this dominant fashion may feel threatened. Sure, they may also find it attractive, but in different settings, such as business, the feelings change. Because women *obviously* don't have the genitals of a man, they are prone to close or cross their legs as a response to males in these positions.

But this doesn't mean women can't respond appropriately. Women who encounter a man constantly 'advertising' his pelvis may counter in a number of ways. Firstly, they can accentuate their own feminine power curves. Secondly, they can subtly mock the male's testosterone-laden display with a witty remark or tone of voice change. And finally, they might approach the man extremely closely, but non-sexually, forcing him to change his posture, lest he be accused of harassment...

A little underhanded, but hey, sometimes you've gotta work what you got.

But remember, it's not even about that. It's not even about what you *got* or what somebody else *got*. It's about your ability to recognize it. And now that we've reviewed some of the more important gestures, postures, positions and movements that you will see in everyday life, you're getting closer.

Now, in most contexts these body language signals mean something similar. Obviously, knowing the distinct people, environments and related factors is critical to decoding what you're seeing—but for the most part, the commonalities remain.

Of course, this is assuming a certain *cultural milieu*. As you probably already know, body language can change drastically depending on where you are, and we will get into those societal and cultural shifts in much greater detail, a little later...

But for now...

Let's assume you are dealing with somebody who is very skilled at showing certain clusters and sending certain signals. Let's assume you don't want simply to observe and react to another person's body language... Let's assume you want to steer, and even *control*, that other person's body language.

Well, guess what? With enough hours of intense, focused, dynamic real-world practice, you can do just that...

It is time to not only recognize the many forms, types and styles of body language communication... It is time to *control* them, before they ever even happen...

The Telepath – How to Read, *Mine* & Hijack the Mind

You might be saying to yourself, that's impossible. Mind-reading? *No way.*

For many of us this is the standard reaction. And frankly, it's totally natural. After all, how many times have we been told that mind-reading is possible, only to find that it's a sham? Smoke and mirrors? An elaborate hoax perpetrated on others for fame and fortune?

How many television shows—scifi, fantasy, dystopian—depict this ability, only to indicate how far fetched from real life it really is?

If you, like many, find mind-reading implausible or downright impossible, you're not alone. However, that doesn't mean it doesn't happen. And that doesn't mean it *can't* happen, for virtually anyone, anywhere, given the requisite foundation.

What many people don't realize is that the mind is the world. Your mind and the way you think, feel, and specifically speak, about the world, can actually *rearrange* the building blocks of that world. You are essentially programming your environment by thinking certain thoughts and expressing those thoughts.

You are establishing boundaries, often without conscious *awareness*, and you are permitting and prohibiting entry, often without conscious *intent*.

You are the restrictions you place on yourself. And many of us, unfortunately, are placing them on ourselves all the time, without ever even realizing it.

To be able to read minds, to be able to analyze and predict and understand and even control minds, we must learn to eradicate these preconceived notions. We must tear down our mental and cognitive barriers, and we must establish new channels, new pathways, new inroads to a larger parapsychological realm.

Your five senses are only the beginning

You must aspire to more, and you must do so in a way that is clear, clean, and consistent. The three Cs. Let these words be your guidance. Allow them to move you forward as you tackle the world with maximum power.

Don't allow others to hold you back. To convince you that are you buying into pseudoscience or malarkey, or that you're some kind of hopeless, self-deluded fool.

These people—*they're* the fools. They have chosen their paths and cloistered their minds. They have already sealed off their brains and their beliefs from the incredible powers of the para-psychic realm.

In many ways, these people are lacking.

But they are not alone. In fact, many of use are lacking, and suffering, as a result of our modern lifestyles. The treat-the-symptom, ignore-the-system mentality of modernized society has taken its toll. We've lost touch with our primal powers. We've ignored one of our most prescient assets, leaving it atrophied and unused, like a muscle we never move.

But this can change. We can once more learn to apply that gifted, incredible, human gateway between the human mind, and the mind of all. We can learn again, to apply the Human Pineal Gland—our Third Eye—for abilities we never *dreamt* possible...

The Gateway –Opening your Pineal Gland for Para-psychic Power

In case you're unaware, the Third Eye (as it's often called) is REAL.

This is not some illusory conception conjured up by weirdos high on psychedelics. This is not some abstract concept defined by crazy philosophers and loony 'psychics.' This is a very real, very measurable, very human, *thing*.

The Third Eye, known more formally as the Pineal Gland, is a powerhouse of human consciousness. It stabilizes us and energizes us. It electrifies our thoughts and feelings, potentially changing, framing and transforming our entire perceptual universe. Many have argued that the Pineal Gland is the pathway to increased extrasensory awareness, to inhuman cognitions, to otherworldly abilities and predispositions.

This isn't pseudoscience, this isn't psycho-babble.

The Pineal Gland is REAL.

But let's get into what exactly this so-called Gland is. Before we can unlock para-psychic powers, before we can even think about truly expanding our comprehension and contortion of reality, we must understand the Pineal Gland. More importantly, we must understand how to *power it up.*

But what *is* this mysterious gland, you ask.

As it turns out, the pineal gland is about the size of a pea, often described as resembling a pine cone. In fact, its name comes from the word *pinea* which actually *means* pine cone. It is located toward the middle of the brain, and has a storied history, according to the mystics and the seers. Although it is largely inactive, it is believed to have one day engaged a number of spiritual, inter-dimensional, holistic abilities.

In fact, the pineal gland has long been described as the connection, or gateway, to and between the human spirit and some greater celestial being. Its history is undoubted. The Greeks believed it governed all of our higher thinking abilities, while others, such as Descartes, contended that it was the centerpiece of the soul.

In this sense, the pineal gland or Third Eye is the *full* vision of the world and allows us to see beyond the pitiful constraints of the five senses.

But this is the ethereal, mystic conception of the Third Eye. Fact is, it also has a very real biological basis. See, the gland is connected to a consistent and necessary release of one of the body and mind's most important hormones: melatonin.

Melatonin is one of the primary controllers of our circadian rhythms, our reproductive abilities, our time perceptions, our stress management, and our ability to readily adapt to new external and internal stressors in this crazy thing called Life.

As it seems, the balance of various elements in this pineal gland affect the way we interpret the way we live. To put it another way, it is a highly active, highly impactful *reality-modulator*. One molecule most influential in this *modulation* of reality, produced and powered by our pineal gland, is dimethyltryptamine (DMT).

In case you didn't know, DMT is one of the world's most *intense* psychoactive molecules in higher doses.

Although used (and likely abused) for thousands of years, DMT was not formally discovered and legitimized until 1936 by a guy named Richard Manske. Of course, at the time it was just a molecule. A chemical. Something with some importance in some form, for some lives. It wasn't until 1956, that DMT was actually understood as a psychoactive agent, documented for its pharmacological components and effects. Some people thought it made you contact aliens. Others, thought it made you die and come back.

Although this may all sound wild and crazy, the fact is: DMT is not crazy. In fact, it's relatively normal. That is, in *normal* doses.

See, in normal, sustenance doses, DMT is nothing more than a regulatory mechanism. A reality checker for our brains. Too much, and we begin to see things that aren't there (schizophrenia), too little, and we don't see enough of what's there (dimness and flatness of experience).

But don't be fooled. DMT is not merely present in humans, in the brain, blood and urine of humans. It is also an important hormone in the body and brain of animals and plants.

And should this come as a surprise? Animals have long been capable of seemingly extrasensory abilities. Plants, meanwhile, have been used (and abused) for their psychedelic properties for thousands of years. As far back as we can recall, humans have recorded the amazing ability of plants—rife with DMT—to unlock new frontiers of consciousness.

Whether it be connecting to perceived higher-level 'entities,' experiencing fantastical visual and auditory hallucinations, establishing so-called seances with the dead, connecting with extraterrestrials, or getting a glimpse of the after-life, DMT has served incredible purposes in incredible ways.

Some have posited that DMT allows us to tap into alternate levels, or tiers, of reality. In this framework, DMT alters the brain chemistry so as to attune us to all sorts of incomprehensible 'frequencies' of perception, allowing us to see otherwise invisible 'actors' behind the curtain of everyday, normal functioning.

Sound crazy?

Well not so fast. This chemical has been noted for these effects by *countless* different peoples and cultures, across the expanse of time.

In certain doses, it *undeniably* allows us to explore all sorts of expansionary realms, permeating barriers and penetrating new territories of mental, cognitive, and spiritual awareness. As researchers have noted, DMT is one of the few chemicals that the human brain actively accepts, unlike certain carbohydrates or fats, which are prohibited from entering. This is crucial. The fact that DMT crosses the blood-brain barrier so easily is testament to its fundamental role in human functioning.

And to many researchers, indispensable to keeping us... 'normal.'

Why is a certain level of DMT normal, you ask?

Because we're human. Because we are wild. Because, as you already know, we are hardwired to enjoy and express and experience all sorts of pleasurable, ecstatic, hedonistic things.

Think back to when you were a kid. Before jobs and bills and kids and spouses and lack of sleep and all the sorts of daily requirements and duties and stressors you've now come to accept as Life.

Think back.

What do you recall? Were you wide-eyed at the world? Were you ready to take on all new ventures, ready to engage anything, willing to float in a certain mind-space where wasting time *wasn't* wasting time, but just living?

Fact is, we are programmed, hardwired, destined to be human. And part of being human, a major part of being human, is enjoying the Moment.

But why is this?

I'll tell you why. Because of our pineal glands! When we're young, we haven't yet been exposed to the many external factors that age us. That deteriorate us. That *calcify* our pineal glands and make us feel as if we're losing our touch with the world.

The simple joys of the world? Fading and washing away...

But this is no surprise.

In fact, sadly, this is basically the norm. See, when we're young, we're green. Before the age of 10, we are basically experiencing a life that is free of major stress, free of the many responsibilities burdening us as adults. As kids, our brains are still like sponges, our wonder at everyday living still at an all-time high. The reason? Because our levels of *DMT* are high, and our pineal glands—not yet calcified!

Fact of the matter is: DMT is everywhere. It's in our brains, our blood, our urine; it's in the plants we smoke and consume; it's in the animals we see and hunt and eat. DMT surrounds us at every corner, influences us in every way, and contributes to our lives in a fashion that many of us have yet to even fathom.

And DMT, in all its wondrous, mysterious glory—is borne from the Pineal Gland. From the 'Third Eye.' From the very thing, the very gland, that makes us human.

But now we have to transcend.

Before we can be *beyond* human, before we can even *dream* of unlocking the full-fledged powers of this supernatural gland, we have to go deeper. We have to learn smarter. We have to engage abilities we thought dormant, lost, impossible, for all this time...

Let's do it.

Let's learn some of the key methods of improving the Pineal Gland, and let's master the art of Third Eye Activation.

Okay.

So the first step is common sense. But it *must* be said. First, we have to be healthy. Not only healthy, but specifically, consistently healthy. In a way, perhaps, that you thought was impossible. We have to enter a different *paradigm* of thought. Concerning life. Concerning the body. Concerning everything you probably *thought* you knew about the human spirit.

Health is not simply about your latest check-up. It's not simply about your reading for this, or your level for that. Health, true health, is about how you feel spiritually.

You don't have to be religious. You just have to have a soul. A reason. A conviction. A higher purpose for your daily, weekly, monthly, yearly, life-time pursuits. You just have to have a reason. That's all. That's it. And frankly, that's *everything*.

If you can give a reason, a purpose, to why you do what you do, then you can live it up. You can succeed for life. You can garner new perspectives and new feelings, and new levels of absolute domination. You can reach a point in which you flow seamlessly. This is a different point. An unconscious point. Of no return. A good point, in which you swear that you've uncovered the meaning of the universe and everything that comes with it.

You think you know the world. And you *do* know the world. That is, when you allow the world to come to you...

So without further ado, let's delve deeper—once more—into the indeterminable depths of the unconscious. It is time to learn how, exactly, you activate your Third Eye...

Easy, Everyday Techniques for Awakening Your Inner Eye

Although our pineal glands become calcified as we age, age alone is not the reason. In fact, it is not the fact that we're getting older, that makes our Third Eyes dim and disappear. It is the fact that we're getting lazier.

What does this mean?

It means we're not doing what we should do. We're not taking the necessary steps. We're allowing our modern lifestyles, our toxic, destructive modern environments, to take us down. Our brain's most perceptive organ, our most important sense of all, is being destroyed.

So we must change. We must unlock the dormant powers of this once mystic, all-seeing eye, and we must do so intelligently and systematically.

When it comes to unleashing the powers of your pineal gland, and seeing others in ways that they cannot see you, there are two things to remember: (1) Decalcifying and (2) Activating.

The first important element, Decalcifying, is about preparing your pineal gland for use. It's about shaking off the years of rust and allowing your pineal gland room to work. It's about awakening the dormant powerhouse inside by giving it the conditions it needs to thrive. The second important step is to actually activate it. Once you have provided your pineal gland a conducive internal environment, you must exercise it.

It's like anything. If you want to be an athlete, you first have to provide your body the proper vitamins, minerals and nutrients it needs, and then you have to use it. The right fuel makes the right fire.

See, the reason the pineal gland calcifies is because of all the toxins, pollutants, contaminants and negative external agents that work internally to 'muck' it up. In order to reverse this damage (decades of damage), we must decalcify. The reason calcification is so bad is that it leads to the formation of phosphate crystals. Your pineal gland will literally harden from these crystals, leading to lower levels of production, and general disturbances in daily functions, such as your circadian wake-sleep cycles, your moods and perceptions, your energy levels, your mental and cognitive abilities—and on and on and on.

Bottom line: it ain't good.
So let's fix it...

Halides: These chemical compounds contain two different elements and are some of the most damaging things we can take into our bodies when it comes to pineal gland health. Although not all halides are bad for us in reasonable amounts (ie; salt), three of them are. This trifecta of 'bad halides' includes flouride, chlorine and bromide.

In case you didn't know, these chemicals are found in all sorts of water, whether our drinking water or the swimming water in our pools. These compounds can also be found in various other forms, whether pesticides, medicines, plastics, soft drinks, and other sorts of 'treatments' to kill potentially risky organisms.

The reason these halides are so dangerous is because they remove the mineral *iodine* from the body. Iodine is absolutely indispensable to overall health. Halides like bromide and flouride and chlorine disrupt the normal regulatory use of iodine, a fundamental fuel for the healthy thyroid.

Because your body does not *naturally* make iodine, exogenous sources of iodine are required. When your thyroid and body and brain are depleted of iodine, you struggle with all sorts of psychological and physical problems. You experience low energy, muddled thought, skin conditions, heart problems, cancers, and general decreases in mood and well-being.

In fact, too much bromide is *so* terrible for your thyroid, body and brain, that is has its own theory of negative consequence, called the Bromide Dominance Theory...

But Bromide is only one of the Terrible Trifecta of Halides. Another, more common, more easily-combated, halide is flouride.

You know flouride. Your dentists tell you you need it. It's in your tap water, in your swimming pools, from seawater, from impurities, from fertilizers, from the processes of various mining, combusting and manufacturing processes. It's all over the place, way more than most people realize.

And it also has terrible consequences for your iodine levels, your body, your brain, and your overall health and well-being. Flouride is known for many deleterious effects and heavily accumulates in the pineal gland. It is yet another reason that our mind-expansion abilities decline so rapidly as we age.

Just think of all the unfiltered water, environmental contaminants, pollutants and toxins you've been exposed to. Don't wanna think about it?

Don't blame ya!

But let's just stop. Take a step back. Think.

Fact is, these chemicals are *not* good for you, and if you don't make the necessary changes now, you never will. Get a water filter, get a filtering shower head, get an ionizer for your pool. And most importantly, combat your iodine deficiency with iodine-rich foods. These include seaweed, tuna, cod, shrimp, tuna and eggs. Also, look into a quality nascent iodine supplement.

You won't notice the effects right away. But after a couple of weeks, your mood will lift, your thoughts will be crisper and cleaner, and your body will feel rejuvenated. More importantly, you might start to feel an almost blissful appreciation for, and connection to, daily life events, situations and circumstances. Your hormone levels will improve as your cells become more adaptive to free radicals and environmental stressors. In most cases, lower doses of nascent iodine supplements will help.

MSM: But halides are just one way our pineal glands become calcified, atrophied, and rendered virtually useless. Another important reason we lose these dormant powers is a lack of something called Methylsulfonylmethane (MSM).

Methylsulfonylmethane (MSM) is a naturally occurring compound often used for alternative medicine. Also known as organic sulfur, it is a readily bio-available, additive-free mineral utilized by the body for normal regulatory functions. It is indispensable to optimizing health and wellness.

But what does it do?

Well, seemingly everything. MSM has been noted for its ability to reduce inflammation, ease joint/muscle pain, limit oxidative stress, and increase antioxidant capacity. In short, it is crucial for affecting many of the base functions of our bodies. It takes care of the simple things first, thus reducing the chances of more complicated diseases and illnesses developing down the road. Simply put, it's absolutely necessary. For baseline health. For baseline vitality. For feeling good now, and 30 years from now. You simply *can't* live without it.

Not to mention its cosmetic effects.

Because MSM is required to produce collagen, our skin can't go without it. When you up your MSM dose, you are building new healthy tissues, fighting off the saggy, leathery, wrinkly effects of natural aging. This collagen-crucial compound also helps with joint and muscle issues, allowing you to be more flexible and quicker to recovery.

As it turns out, MSM is easily absorbed. Although it can be found in natural unprocessed foods, it is often quickly dissipated during cooking, and quickly consumed by the body, preventing future storage. Therefore, we need to consistently ingest it. Sure, it can be obtained from fruits, vegetables, grains, tea, coffee and even beer—but not well. You would need to eat extraordinarly large amounts of food to obtain optimal levels. This is why MSM supplementation is so important. Just be sure to take with plenty of purified water (no tap!) and prepare for incredible detoxification effects! Also, feel free to combine with juiced raw lemon. Organic lemons are great for detoxifying the pineal gland.

Garlic: Another great food item for your pineal gland is the one that is not great for your breath. That's right, every Italian food lover's favorite ingredient! The best garlic is black garlic because it rids your body of calcium deposits while also maintaining its well-researched immunomodulatory effects. Simply use a high-citrus drink to remove the garlic breath. Black garlic may also have antioxidant effects that maintain working memory and cognitive functioning in the prefrontal cortex.

Neem extract: Neem (Azadirachta indica) is a plant known through the ages for its effects as a powerful antioxidant, combating free radicals, preventing the development of diseases, and even potentially <u>modulating the molecular</u>

pathways that contribute to cancer. Although gaining traction in recent years as a naturopathic remedy, neem extract has been frequently used by the Chinese, Ayurvedic, and Unani medicine systems for countless years.

Vitamin K2: Originally termed 'Activator X' by Weston Price in 1945, this compound is now known as Vitamin K2. This incredibly potent vitamin-like game-changer has a whole slew of benefits. Perhaps its most important is the apparent ability to decalcify the arteries and other parts of the body, thus reducing the thickening and hardening of the veins (arteriosclerosis) and the organs. This allows for the redirection of calcium to its rightful place, the bones. Not to mention the energizing of vitamin and mineral absorption. Oh, and K2 has also shown promising results in the prevention of cancers, namely liver and prostate.

The good thing about K2 is that it can be contained naturally from foods such as liver, egg yolks, cheese and butter—from grass-fied cows—and also from sauerkraut and shellfish. Just be sure that you get your meat sources from mostly grass-fed animal fats and fermented foods, as these are richest in K2. Overall, 2 is good for your facial structure, your bones, your teeth, your nervous system, your immune system, and your cardiovascular functioning. Basically, it's good for everything!

Melatonin: As previously discussed, melatonin is produced by your pineal gland and is the primary regulator of our wake-sleep cycles, our reproductive capabilities, our time-space perceptions, our stress responses, and our general ability to withstand the free radicals of daily life changes. Melatonin keeps us feeling 'normal' and in touch with reality. It also allows us to perceive the more vibrant nuances of life with greater vigor and vitality—a result of decalcification of the pineal gland. Many people take melatonin to fall asleep regularly. You can also activate your natural melatonin levels by eating foods. Foods high in tryptophan such as fish are especially important. As it turns out, tryptophan is a precusor to serotonin, a crucial neurotransmitter, which is a precursor to melatonin. Coupling these foods with chamomile tea is also a popular practice for those looking to reduce stress and foster relaxation and rest.

Zeolites: In case you've never heard of these *otherworldly* minerals, you're in for a surprise! Zeolites are naturally occurring crystals, oftentimes located in rocks and clay across the world. In fact, as far back as we can document, cultures and societies have consumed clay for myriad health benefits. Whether animals or humans, these powerful crystals have supercharged the body and mind for many years to date.

The beauty of zeolites is their versatility. They can be used in material preparation for various job sites, in the purification of water, and even in agricultural and medicinal realms of use.

Zeolites work because they detoxify in numerous ways. Not only do they balance pH levels inside our bodies, but they also attenuate allergy symptoms, boost antioxidants, aid digestive enzymes, and cleanse our body of dangerous metals. Zeolites are even believed to eliminate toxic metals, such as lead, without depleting other vital components of the body, such as electrolytes. In other words, they are one of the most efficient detoxifiers known to man.

The reason zeolites work so well is that they actually have a strong magnetism. They literally suck out and hold onto many toxins and harmful organisms. Everything from lead to aluminium, to arsenic and mercury. Zeolites remove these dangerous metals from the tissues and allow them to pass through the body's wastes. By removing the metals, zeolites break down many of the calcium deposits that hold these metals, especially those calcium deposits in the pineal gland. Zeolites are so powerful, they even attack tumors and cancer cells!

Beets: Eat beets and feel great. The reason beets are so powerful is because of mostly one ingredient: boron. Boron is a trace mineral and micronutrient with wide-ranging, deeply-penetrating benefits for all plants, animals and humans. In fact, boron has been found to have so many positive effects, it's almost embarrassing that more people don't know them!

Let's quickly cover these awesome, scentifically-founded, effects: (a) the development of skeletal structure, (b) the improvement of cellular processes in healing, (c) the increasing of the body's use of estrogen, testosterone, and various vitamins, (d) the boosting of magnesium absorption, (e) the reduction of inflammatory responses, (f) the increasing of antioxidant effectiveness, (g) the improvement of electro-chemical activity in the brain, (h) the prevention and treatment of numerous cancers (lung, cervical, lymphoma, etc.), and (i) the reduction of chemotherapy side effects.

In case all of this isn't enough, boron also removes flouride from the body and brain, thus drastically delaying, preventing and/or reducing the withering of your pineal gland. In case you are looking to skip the supplement Borax and obtain boron more naturally—it's easy! You don't even have to eat beets. You can consume almonds, walnuts, avocados, broccoli, chick peas, red grapes, red apples and raisins.

Not too bad, right?

Tamarind: You've likely heard of this one. It comes from the tamarind tree and can be used in all sorts of teas, extracts and exotic concoctions. It is a staple in Ayurvedic circles, and considered an alternative medicine by many people and peoples across the world. The main reason tamarind is good for your pineal gland (aside from its well-known health benefits) is that it expedites excretion of flouride through the urine.

So enjoy tamarind. Take in the good stuff and piss away the crap!

Nigella Sativa: Considered by many to be a 'miracule herb,' these obsidian black rectangular seeds have been extensively studied. The seeds contain a number of unusual bioactive components, in addition to numerous amino acids, vitamins, minerals, and other dietary constituents. In Islamic culture, Nigella Sativa is considered the premiere form of healing medicine. In case you doubt that these little seeds actually work, look no further than their innumerable scientifically-supported benefits. These "include antidiabetic, anticancer, immunomodulator, analgesic, antimicrobial, anti-inflammatory, spasmolytic, bronchodilator, hepato-protective, renal protective, gastro-protective, antioxidant properties."

Now, in case you're wondering how to reap this amazing spectrum of effects, don't worry. You also have a spectrum of *consumption* methods. You can eat the black seeds by themselves, mixed with a little flavor like honey, boiled, in warm milk, ground up and swallowed, sprinkled on your desserts or breads or pastries, or even inhaled as incense.

So enjoy. Swallow well, chew good, or breathe nice and deep and inhale. Nigella Sativa is here to help.

Chaga Mushroom: These mushrooms may look like something out of a weird scifi world, but in reality, they're everything you want and more. Considered the most nutrient dense of all known tree growths, these mushrooms are valued by many Asian cultures to be the dominant *jewel* of the plant kingdom. The reason these mushrooms are so enriched with 'goodies' is because they must survive against all odds, in the harshest, most unforgiving of climates.

One of the most powerful component of these 'shrooms is melanin, the key product providing pigment for our eyes, skin and hair. Melanin is also a critical antioxidant, critical to our pineal gland, and critical to regulating our wake-sleep cycles, our restorative powers, and our reality-testing capabilities.

However, chaga mushroom are most known for their antioxidant abilities. Antioxidants are important because they combat what is commonly called oxidative stress. In general, this stress relates to the way our bodies and minds handle the plethora of external and internal variables, often called 'free radicals.' Basically, oxidative stress is the way our bodies rust and deplete, and can only be countered by the way our bodies react and repair. Some people's bodies naturally repair and heal better. They live foolish, unhealthy lives and rarely suffer severe consequences until much later in age. Other people may live far more healthily, but their body's natural abilities are weak—and free radicals may cause immune disorders, cancers, and so on.

Which is why chaga mushrooms are so critical. They fight DNA damage across your body, help repair the most minute deterioriations, and help detoxify everything from your immune system to your pineal gland. Oh, and did I mention they are great for ulcers, blood pressure, viruses, sicknesses, diabetes, and general pain and discomfort? Check. Them. Out.

But in the end, chaga mushrooms are just another food. Another edible item that helps clear your head, heart, body and soul of destructive toxins.

Sometimes, decalcifying can be done *without* ingesting something, or taking something, or drinking down the latest greatest elixir of power. Sometimes, all you need is a little meditation. Become mindful, learn how to <u>harmonize your inner calm</u>. Strive to minimize sugar, salts and fat. Learn <u>neurogenic dieting</u>. Train to get up early, to watch the sun. Learn **sungazing** to absorb the almighty powers that make us. We are, after all, born from stardust, are we not?

In fact, sungazing (aside from yoga and meditation) is probably the most powerful activity for pineal gland decalcifying. It's also probably the easiest. As long as you can get up early enough, or arrange your schedule to be outside at the right location and time, then you're golden. Rising sun or setting sun. Preferably both. You'll notice the effects, often minor, but sometimes *highly* anomalous.

The main thing to remember about this occult practice is that many mystics *swear* it's a cure-all for holistic wellness. Although detractors will point to its tenuous scientific basis, many anecdotes support the efficacy of sungazing...

Still, the debate rages on.

So far, most evidence is considered either pseudoscience or dangerous quackery. Critics claim that it's impossible to absorb the sun's 'energies' simply by staring at it. They argue that doing so will result in solar retinopathy. They argue that doing so will make you lose your sight. That doing so is stupid, unfounded, pointless, and generally the practice of wanna-be shamans who know not what they preach.

And the proponents *fire* back. In their estimations, sungazing is a *panacea*. It cures everything from mood disorders to general anxiety to more serious, debilitating illnesses such as neuropathy, muscular dystrophy and cancer. Their reasons are manifold. Firstly, they claim that the sun is somehow filtered through their eyes. Although (obviously) humans are not plants—and cannot create chlorophyll—we are still capable of somehow processing the stardust 'core' of the sun's energies, seen and unseen. Many 'gazers' have expressed a renewed ability to recover, sleeping less, feeling better, and requiring far fewer meals.

Although the scientific evidence for such claims is lacking, it is not entirely absent. In fact, there *are* a number of correlations between the use of sunlight and the pineal gland's functioning and capabilities. For instance, the Third Eye, as it were, is *very* useful for engaging a number of important faculties.

Remember: the pineal gland is directly tied to light. Its main function is to release melatonin. It regulates sleep-wake cycles and allows for the body to regularly experienve reality. Many of our pineal glands are underactive because they are simply deprived of natural light. They are exposed to all sorts of *artifical* lights, gadgets, computers, and devices, and are not privy to the kinds oflight that we actually require. Once the main fuel of the pineal gland is supplied (natural light), it begins to do what it was meant to.

Remember, the science for sungazing is lacking but not absent. It is there, and it is real. It is important because it allows us to engage our faculties to their fullest potential. Some resarchers have posited that sungazing allows sunlight to enter through the retinal-hypothalamic tract, before direclty affecting the brain. It is hypothezied that this stimulates the pineal gland, thus increasing the regular secretion of melatonin and serotonin, the two main hormones in our ability to feel 'normal' and 'good.'

But sungazing is no easy task. If you don't abide by the important rules, the dictates of the ancients, then you are likely going to experience many of the terrible consequences the ancient speak of. In fact, many of these effects are terrible because they affect us in a way that is not only detrimental to our holistic mental, physical and emotional health, but also reprehensible in an environmentally-friendly world.

So here's what you need to do. You need to sungaze at the right time and in the right way. You need to do it in a way that is *grounded*. You need to have your feet on the ground (literally) and barefoot. This allows you to act as a conduit between the powerful energies you will be intaking and the other multifarious energies you will counterbalancing and handling throughout your daily adventures. In other words, stand barefoot *on the earth*. Proponents and practitoners of sungazing suggest that you only stare either one hour after sunrise, or one hour before *sunset*. The main factor to consider is that you have to be able to engage in direct ocular sunlight. If you have some sort of medical condition such as cataracts or retinal deterioration, do not—I repeat DO NOT—do this.

Be sure that you are fully physically and psychologically ready to engage in this activity. Otherwise you are screwed... and I mean that. I'm not playing games. You also have to have your mindset in a certain stage where you are ready to *fully* accept the ethereal energies of the sun. You can't simply stand there as if this is nothing. You have to be ready to fully engage the most powerful star in our immediate world, and you have to do so with a willingness, acceptance, and gratitude that *creates*, partially, the placebo effect you seek. Once you have attuned your mind, body and spirit to channeling this primordial energy for the benefit, then you are ready to actually receive it adaptively.

Okay, so here are the rules: you have to do it for 10 seconds. Just 10 seconds the first time. And then you can do it for 10 more and 10 more and 10 more, the second and third days.

Only increase by (at most) 10 seconds per day. If you do anymore, you will run the risk of solar retinopahy, corneal damage, and other terrible, life-altering, debilitating conditions.The importance is building up a resilience, tolerance, resistance, whatever you want to call it. Basically, you are learning to 'ingest' or incorporate the sun's rays in a way that is adaptive to your general health and well-being. You are learning how to accept this solar energy in a way that is not only important to how you go about your daily activities, but integral to how you see, perceive, and experience your daily life.

If you miss a day, even just one, you must re-calibrate your sungazing window. Subtract 10 seconds for every day that you miss. Ten seconds is all it takes. You must do this to readjust your eyes and brain to the absorption of highly powerful (and potentially damaging) rays. So if you sungaze for 4 days, and are able to gaze for 40 uninterrupted seconds on the fourth day—but then miss two days—you should resume sungazing for only 20 seconds the next time.

Be careful to observe your bodily cues. Do not simply sungaze without knowing how long, or for what reason, or at what time, you are engaging. Be sure to notice how you feel. Your eyes may water, your eyes may hurt—so stop! If you close your eyes, blink multiple times, and the after-image is still there for a prolonged time—you've gone too far!

Learn from your mistakes. Do not be discouraged if you overdo it one time or multiple times. Always err on the side of caution and gaze only for as long as you feel comfortable.

If you are not yet ready to engage the sun full-on, begin with another source of light. Try, first, looking directly at a fire pit or candle flame. The trick is to look at natural light in a way that you're not used to. If you don't want to start with these things, then start with the sun. But instead of looking *at* it, look *toward* it. Look in the general direction, not focusing on the sun, but the area around it. You can also focus on the moon, which is a good practice for those seeking a skyward source of light.

Remember, the entire point of sungazing is to decalcify your pineal gland. You are returning to the source, the source of all of us—stardust. You are tapping into a primoridal, ethereal energy. Your intentions and feelings going in are crucial. How you feel and think about this practice dictates, to large extent, how you will gain from it. Placebo effect is powerful. Do not approach sungazing as something to be overcome or won. You are not doing it to be tough or push through.

It is a type of meditation. A type of mystic celebration. Again, sungazing has been linked to increased levels of hormones in the brain. To larger pineal glands, to greater, more natural balances between body and mind. And more generally, to improved mood and vitality.

Give it a try. Keep an open mind. And see where sungazing takes you.

Gearing Up: Top Ways to PREPARE your Personal Psychological Warfare

Okay.

So now we've covered many of the factors at play in decalcifying your Pineal Gland, the primary gateway to supersensory perceptions and performance.

Now what?

Well, before we can fully master the art of these enhanced psychological powers, we must activate them. Once you have fully cleansed yourself of contaminants and toxins, and things like flouride, chlorine adn bromide, you are ready to begin awakening your pineal gland.

Remember, this will take some time and practice. And before you can use it outright on a whim, you have to use it consciously, consistently, and proactively.

Let's cover some of the most critical activators for awakening your Third Eye.

Firstly, accept your current state. Acceptance of <u>The Moment</u> is critical to knowing where you stand, and where you must eventually go (assuming you wish to improve). Some of us have various problems that are pronounced and disruptive. Many of us have numerous smaller problems that come together to create different bigger problems. And some of us have just one or two problems that are so monstrous, they consume our lives.

Know your problems, and know how they relate to the previous state of your pineal gland. Now that your pineal gland has been reasonably decalcified, you will better understand how you once were. It may be like awakening from a dream, emerging from a haze, stepping out from a darkness that you never knew existed.

For instance, some of us are lacking. We are deficient. Our disordered thoughts, feelings and behaviors have caused us to embrace, or accept, a lifestyle that is not conducive to optimal living. An optimized Third Eye does not cause us to be excessively wild or sedated. It is a reality balance. If you are lacking in pineal energies, you are likely overly passive, emotionally sensitive, fearful, and lazy. If you have an excess of pineal energies, you are probably arrogant, manipulative, bipolar, dogmatic, or overly controlling. However, if you are balanced in your energies (and everybody has their own *individual* balance), you are likely able to handle both the yin and yang of life. In other words, you are both open and shut to forces at bay.

You will accept help and support, but you will not rely on it. You will assert yourself in situations for personal gain and for the gain of others, but you will not dominate simply for dominance's sake. You seek to better yourself, but not to belittle others. You seek a contentmnent, happiness, ultimate understanding beyond yourself, beyond material things, beyond base desires like food, drink and sex. You do not need somebody else to feel whole or right, but you like being with others. Perhaps you do want a partner, but your partner does not encapsulate you.

Knowing your pineal powers is also critical to explaining your physical and mental issues. People with energy deficiencies of the pineal gland may find themselves constantly baffled. They may have dull senses, cloudy thoughts, and general lethargy of body and mind. They may suffer from depression, dull aches and pains, and general discomfort. By and large, their bodies do not work fluidly.

However, when your energies are overloaded, you simply cannot control them. You are prone to overexercise. You are a glutton, a fiend. You do everything to an extreme. You seek pleasure to the point that pleasure is pain. Your body responds by hurting in acute, undeniable ways. You overcompensate. You overtalk, overwork, overstep your bounds more than others. And you apologize far less frequently. You may have delusions, hallucinations. You oftentimes lose sense of reality. You may be an egomaniac, a narcissist. Obsessed with material things, obsessed with how you look, obsessed with how others perceive you to the point that it dominates your life. You spend inordinate amounts of time, inordinate amounts of energy on things that oftentimes fall flat. You don't work efficiently, you work excessively. You don't think realistically, you think drastically.

You are, in every way, shape and form, a problem to yourself and to others. And in many ways, you don't even know it. Usually, because you won't dare allow yourself to.

Now, for most of us, we won't exist on the extremes. We'll be somewere on the spectrum, slightly closer to one pole than the other. We might see ourselves on both sides, at times, with a general predispositon toward one set of traits than another.

Okay, good.

Now let's get into the deeper stuff. Now that you've reached a point where you understand yourself through metacognitions—*you think about your thinking*—now you're reaching a point where you can evolve. Improve. Transcend to a higher plane of reality awareness. If you become skilled, truly skilled, you can even embrace various aspects of both extremes, adaptively.

After all, life does throw us curve balls. And sometimes, it's bad to be milquetoast. Sometimes, we have to fully go one way or the other, take an extreme stand and fight for what we need. Sometimes, we have to do it with all the powers in the world.

Sometimes, we have to use psychological warfare to get… it… done.

This is critical. Warfare doesn't necessarily mean you are destroying someone, or even hurting someone. Sometimes it does. But remember, warfare can also be intelligence-based, psychological, and/or mental. Remember, many intelligence agencies use cyber warfare and propaganda warfare to change minds. Although the argument can be made that this is manipulation or subtle coercion, others will argue that it is, in fact, 'good' for the manipulated people. Sometimes, they are manipulated simply to be used and abused. Other times, they are being 'converted' to a better way, physically unhurt but mentally changed.

So be wary. Consider your uses for your own psychological warfare. You may, just may, have to hurt a bad person, even a good person—which is *okay*. The moral dilemma is on you. Just be sure you have thought it through clearly and intelligently. And be sure, no matter what you do, that you stand resolute in your decision.

There is nothing worse than a mind full of friction with a heart without conviction.

So don't be left to your own, faulty devices.

Optimize them. Transform them. Make them work for you in the way you want, when you want, how you want, for the gains and goals you want.

And many times, those goals involve people. In order to use your pineal gland for psychological warfare, it is important to first understand the thinking and feeling of the people you target.

First, consider the predominant thought process style of the individual(s) you target. Generally, we can define thinking as either conceptual or procedural. As you might have guessed, conceptual thinkers view the overall idea or abstract notion of things. They see the forest for the trees. They might not understand all the creatures and insects and plants and organisms living inside the forest, but they generally understand the relationships, why they are important, and how they continue. The procedural thinker, by contrast, savors the details. He or she will see the trees for the forests, aware of all the excruciating details but, perhaps, unaware of the larger forest and its role in the world.

You can often tell how somebody predominantly thinks just based on speech patterns. If somebody is a conceptual thinker, he or she will talk more broadly and less frequently. Consider a conversation about a new friend. The conceptual thinker might refer to this new male friend as *'this guy'* or *'my new friend.'* Meanwhile, the procedural thinker will refer to the new male friend as *'my newest friend John, a carpenter'* or *'My old stockbroker friend Sam'*...

Basically, the details matter and increase the length of the speech. There is less generality for the procedural thinker and more abstractness for the conceptual thinker.

The reasons for these differences in thought and speech are directly tied to the two hemispheres of the brain. As neuroscience has shown repeatedly, the right hemisphere is far more intuitive, emotionally intelligent and impulsive, and will explain thoughts and feelings in terms of sensing and feeling, whereas the left hemisphere is more apt to use analytical thought and logic-based deductions and inductions to ascertain a 'solution.'

Right-brained people also may seem to act randomly, are more likely to be artistic, and—because the right side controls the left side of the body—are more likely to be left-handed.

Of course, this is an oversimplification. Research shows that the left brain and right brain work together. They communicate. And one without the other will not be nearly as strong. That said, the brain *has* been shown to transfer abilities typically associated with one side to other parts. This neuroplasticity is an incredible testament to the adaptability of the brain. Different functions can be handled, managed, and compensated for by other regions. The brain is an amazing thing.

But just think about the importance of both sides. A person might be considering stock options. The right-brained person might take a big-picture view, thinking that the stock will rise from a gut feeling based on the direction things 'seem' to be heading. Meanwhile, a left-brained person might take a detail-oriented approach, thinking *'based on these quarterly performances and projections, the trajectory is x, y, z.'*

Now consider when both hemispheres are working in concert. The individual not only has an intuitive sense or feel of the stock forecasts, but can support that feeling with hard stats and projections. Pretty good!

Even victims of brain trauma can make use of both sides of the brain, or new parts of the brain, to compensate for the injuries. Essentially, skills and abilities previous attributed to one part, lobe, region or hemisphere are now rerouted, and rewired, through "adaptive changes on both a structural and functional level, ranging from molecular, synaptic, and cellular changes to more global network changes."

Overall, however, there are several important *brain-inclinations* to remember. If you can understand the *brain-inclinations* of your target, you can better harbor psychological warfare against that target.

Logicians – this brain inclination is heavily left-leaning. As such, it is strictly adherent to logic, reasoning and facts. Feelings are largely disregarded in favor of practical explanations and solutions. Math and science are considered the holy grail, and other more intuitive approaches are typically regarded as inferior. Details are precious to the logician, and you will notice right away by the way they talk and behave. Methodical expressions include saying things such as, *"We should proceed"* or *"Let us analyze"* or by using adverbs literally such as *"therefore," "thus," "henceforth," "thereby,"* and so on.

The Experiential – Although open to *new* experiences, they are inclined toward learning and knowledge gained from experience and experience only. They would rather live it, than read about it in a book. They will apply empiricism in a logical manner according to left-brained tendency, but are not opposed to embracing current, unexpected situations, settings and circumstances.

The experiential relies heavily on the five senses. The senses are considered the end-all-be-all of existence, and other faculties believed or unknown (such as the Third Eye) are disregarded. If something new happens, the experiential will only believe what he or she already knows, and can know, from the five senses.

The Dreamer – You know this type. Head in the clouds, feet, somewhere, meandering on the ground. This type is so predominantly right-brained, they barely touch the earth. You wonder if they've ever even heard of the word "logic." The Dreamer will often seem detached or unaware, likely due to his or her detachment from reality. Although the Dreamer has profound intuitions about broad, abstract concepts, the day-to-day details are lost. The Dreamer is the nutty professor who can't tie his shoes. The disorganized writer who forgets to eat. The strange hermit who spends time along and barely interacts with people in the daily world.

You can tell the Dreamer by the way he or she talks too. The Dreamer will often speak very little, with uncertain, quiet words. Or, the Dreamer may speak in disconnected fashion, long-winded and all over the place. The Dreamer's words will be hard to follow, and harder to dissect. Sometimes, you don't even try.

The Ideologue – Like the Dreamer, the Ideologue is largely motivated by intuition and feeling. The right brain thinking is evident from the very beginning. The Ideologue will approach life through the lens of ideology. Certain events, situations, ideas, concepts and even facts will be filtered through that lens. Those 'data points' that do not meet these criteria may be omitted, skewed, rejected, challenged, or totally changed to align with the current ideological lens.

The main characteristic of the Ideologue is confirmation bias. The Ideologue will seek information that confirms preexisting beliefs and notions. Information that does not adhere to these beliefs will not be actively sought. Diverse viewpoints and opinions may be deemed illegitimate for this reason.

Even when confronted with incontrovertible facts and evidence, the Ideologue may state simply, *"I don't believe that"* or *"That doesn't seem right"* or *"I don't feel that's correct."* The Ideologue, by and large, will 'log' perceptions and judgments that are ideologically sound, and reject those that are not. The preferred ideology of the Ideologue will be a product of environment, history, and personal and interpersonal factors.

And these factors are critical.

Because not only do they affect how the Ideologue thinks and feels, they affect how we all think and feel. And our types of thoughts and feelings may change. *Obviously* each type is not mutually exclusive. We all naturally display characteristics from every type, some more than others. Some of us are mostly one way, others take a little of this with a little of that. In order to find out what your target prefers, pose open-ended questions. Start generally and allow for specificity to come naturally.

What matters is how you use it. If you seek to truly decode another person's mind, to mold that mind or manipulate that mind, as you see fit, you need to be able to talk the talk. But more than anything, you need to be able to recognize. Recognize the person you're dealing with.

And understand, that there is no such thing as hemispheres. That's right.

After *everything* just previously said, forget 'hemisphere.' Your decalcified Third Eye does not know hemispheres. It knows oneness. It knows vastness. It knows the infinite powers of an interconnected, holistic, integrated consciousness. You are not divided, you are united.

But the people you target… the targets of your psychological warfare? Most likely, they are not united. They are existing in a sub-par, calcified state. Their pineal glands are atrophied, and their brains are more segmented. Broken down. Divided up. Not working as seamlessly in tandem, but fighting internally. Not consistently. Not effectively.

Most people are a mess.

Which is why you, as the mind-reader, as the master of psychological warfare, need to clean up the mess.

You need to provide order from chaos. More importantly, you need to provide the *illusion* of order.

You must provide a solution. Multiple solutions. In fact, you must introduce the problems, for which you already *have* the solutions. There are a number of ways to do this. And all of them require a seemingly harmless conversation. Once you get talking you can get learning. So talk the talk, the way you were meant to. Use these conversational tactics today, to begin permeating the mind of your chosen target:

The Replica

This is a subtle tactic used to plant the seed in your target's mind. What's the seed?
The seed is the belief that you, somehow, in some way, are understanding the person on a deeper level. Not just

understanding, but actually predicting, their thoughts and actions.

The beauty of this exercise is that by creating the illusion that you are reading thoughts, you will actually be able to essentially read thoughts. A self-fulfilling prophecy. A placebo effect. Whatever you wish to call it, the conditions will create the outcome.

Let's delve a little deeper…

Firstly, you have to recognize an undeniable human truth. People like to talk. More than talk, they like to talk about themselves. *Hey we all think we're awesome.* We go about our lives, think about our problems, and oftentimes forget that millions, if not billions, of others are sharing similar struggles, triumphs, etc.

By and large, we are self-centered creatures. Sure, we want to help others at times, maybe even oftentimes, but that doesn't mean we aren't concerned about ourselves. Like, a lot. Like, most of the time.

And it's not a bad thing.

Modern life demands it. We have our bills to pay. Our jobs to worry about. Our homes to tend to. Our family and friends to see. We think about how we could be better, feel better, think better, live better. Exercise. Food. Sleep. Sex. Relationships. Thoughts, moods, feelings, behaviors. We are a product of the environments we inhabit, the efforts we make, the people we surround ourselves with—etc.

Bottom line: we are focused on ourselves.

And this is why **The Replica** is crucial.

When using The Replica, you need to initially listen. Listen to how people communicate their recent experiences. They might talk about who they saw, what happened, what they've been doing, an event, or place or circumstance on their mind or of relevance. They might mention certain proper nouns, the names of people, places and things. They might mention things casually while going into more detail about other things they really find important.

Notice all of these… 'things.'

Then, when it is your turn to respond, don't mention them at all. That's right, act like you never heard them. In fact, talk about stuff that is entirely unrelated, about your own recent happenings and events. Talk for several minutes at least, and then go back.

Bring back up what your target was talking about. All those persons, place and things. Except, *except*, don't use the same words. Use alternate words that sound like what they were talking about. Mention these things in casual fashion. For instance you might say, *"there was this rude guy at the grocery store,"* after the person had told you about some *"weird gentleman"* at *"Safeway."* You might reference bits and pieces of what your target said, but without the proper names.

Although this all sounds rather plain and unimpressive, it is crucial. The trick is to provide as close to a 'replica' of what the person said, without making it obvious. You don't want to simply regurgitate what he or she said. You need to change the details slightly, and make it seem as if you somehow just knew it. Make it seem like it was your experience. Your awareness.

This preys on the basic human instinct to connect. Children often echo what others say. It is a social conditioning tool that allows us to integrate from a very young age, and to make sense of the world. It is integral to normal development, and it is also integral to forming relationships. If you can combine this skill with mirroring body language, not only will you naturally attune to others' sensibilities, but you will win their approval too. This mirroring of body language will even allow you and the other individual to produce greater shared facts, observations and insights, as creativity is maximized through synchronous body language.

The trick is to time your mirroring with your use of The Replica. Initially, as you are simply listening, use body language that is not mirroring, but open. It doesn't matter if your target is shut down, contracted, expressive, loose and limber—whatever. Simply remain in an open, assertive position while listening, as this increases likeability, and then switch to mirroring behaviors once you active The Replica. In the end, you are successfully preparing your target for what comes next (without your target knowing), before planting the verbal seed.

Essentially, you are lowering their barriers. You are overriding their conscious mind and reorienting their *sub*conscious mind. This will allow you to more easily permeate their psyche later on, if you so choose.

The Superlative

Everybody likes a compliment. Some of us more than others. Some of us, rarely need them or want them. Many of us may even feel like too many compliments, or certain compliments, are harmful, that we should be embarrassed or feel guilty.

Others among us, feel that there are never enough compliments. That constant flattery is not only warranted, but required. Some people thrive on compliments, even need them all the time just to get through the day. Other people only need them from time to time...

But all of us, no matter how much we think we don't need them or want them, benefit from compliments.

Why? Easy. They bolster our self-esteem. They keep us going. Keep us working, trying, striving, feeling better when our spirits are low. Propel us forward when life attempts to hold us back.

Simply put, flattery is nice. And it works. In some cases, wonders.

But flattery only works when it's true. Or at least partially true.

See, most people know when you're selling them a line of bull: *"You're the most amazing, incredible, outstanding, lovely perfect little human being on this—"*

No.

When flattery works it works because you have nuggets of truth, garnished with elements of hyperbole. But more importantly, you use generality. Using generality is about saying something that really, frankly, applies to anyone, but in a way that makes it seem like it applies specifically to the individual you target.

But generality is only good if it is flattering generality. Sure, it may be a generality that *'there are a lot of bad people in the world,'* but that doesn't exactly help if you say to somebody, *'like a lot of people, you're bad.'*

So use a positive generality. And start with that generality.

In beginning The Superlative, start with a character trait you know to be generally acceptable. This could be anything from *nice, intelligent, thoughtful, caring* to *friendly, trustworthy, motivated* and/or *attractive*. Differentiate your use of these traits based on the gender. Assuming you are in western culture, men will likely prefer more power-based adjectives, such as 'industrious' or 'successful' or 'pragmatic' and women will prefer more sensitivity-based adjectives, such as 'compassionate' or 'intuitive' or 'perceptive.'

Once you have selected your trait, introduce the generality. Target your individual by saying *'you'* or even supplying the name first: *'John, you...'*

From there, make the superlative. *'John, you're a very pragmatic person...'*

Now stop.

Now it's time to counterbalance. Since you can't simply smother somebody with flattery, you need to show that you're not a brown noser. Use a little negativity. This balance shows that you are not exaggerating or trying to appease. It also makes the statement seem more specific, because you're providing an exception.

For instance: *"John, you're a really pragmatic guy, but sometimes you need to follow your heart instead of your head."* or *"John, you're a really pragmatic guy, but occasionally you struggle with decision-making."*

You can even inject some lightheartedness to make the statement more digestible: *"John you're a really pragmatic guy, but I've heard you sometimes get a little crazy!"*

The point is to get people to digest what you say, and to feel as if a largely generalized statement is not only tailored toward them, but revealing of them. That you, somehow, know something personal about them, and are now imparting that important insight *to* them.

It is also important to react in real-time. You need to gauge the body language. Remember: if they close off, they may be rejecting what you're saying, if they display self-touch, they may be considering it or distracting from it, and if they appear more open, they're likely receiving and accepting your statement.

So react, and adjust accordingly. Let's imagine you say, *"Sarah, you're a tough girl..."*

Then what happens?

Does Sarah tense up? Does she frown? Does she sway or appear to distance herself ever slightly? If Sarah appears to be rejecting or debating your statement, continue differently.

For instance: *"Sarah, you're a tough girl"* – she scrunches her face in doubt – *"in a quiet way that I really respect."* Or: *"Sarah, you're a tough girl"* – she looks offended – *"but you have a soft side that is just incredible."*

The trick is to balance a negative and a positive. If the person reacts negatively, you counter with a positive. If they react positively, you counter negatively.

For instance: *"John, you always seem to have a positive attitude"* – he looks you in the eye with a smile – *"but sometimes it's a little unrealistic."* Or: *"John, your work ethic is absolutely stellar"* – he exposes his wrists with a nod – *"even if it does consume a lot of time."*

In all of these statements, you are trying to come across as intelligent, as perceptive, as fair, and as knowledgeable. You don't want to seem too negative, or overly flattering. You merely want to seem truthful.

But truth has many forms. And probably the best way, the most powerful, omniscient way of permeating the conscious mind of a target, is by targeting the *collective* mind of mankind. What does this mean? It means appealing to the human spirit. The human experience. The archetypes that have traced our historical tracks for centuries and millennia to date.

This involves not just the human condition, but the human condition*ing*. That is, the events, settings, circumstances, situations and unifying experiences that we can all understand, that each and every person—regardless of culture or upbringing—can relate to.

So use it. Target your target and penetrate the subconscious by catching the conscious mind off guard. Enter their mind in a way like no others.

And that all begins with stages…

If you can appeal to the many stages of life that we all endure, then you can appeal to your target. You can win him or her over, gain insights, and penetrate subconsciously. When penetrating the psyche of your target, you have a number of different stages you can address.

The Stages

The Awakening – This stage of human life refers to that period that most of us cannot remember. We were babies, infants, literally physically dependent upon caretakers and caregivers to survive. We need food, we need drink, and more times than not, we need a big ol' napkin to wipe away our mess.

In fact, the main thing any baby does is make a mess. If it's not vomiting, it's spitting. If it's not spitting, it's crying. Or peeing. Or pooing.

Basically, it about managing a tiny incapable human being.

So relate. If you are talking to a person you know who has a kid, use appropriate language. If it's a new parent, plant the relevant seeds. You don't even have to mention the infant or newborn at home. Instead, subtly address that reality without mentioning it explicitly

Depending upon the context, you may say something like, *"It's a **crying** shame"* or *"somebody should **take care** of that **mess**"* or *"such a **bundle** of joy"* or a *"**little ray** of sunshine"* or *"what a **little crybaby**"* or *"the start of a **new life**"*- the trick is to weigh your target's body language and demeanor. If he or she seems more negative, employ a more negative reference, followed by a positive one. If he or she seems more positive, use a more positive reference, followed by a negative one. The goal is to soften up the conscious mind, to elicit emotions, and to permeate the subconscious.

For instance, you might say to the negative parent of a newborn (who you know to be dealing with a hectic life) something like this, about something seemingly unrelated such as work: *"Yea, coworkers can be tough, sometimes it's like you have to **do everything for them**. But eventually they **grow up** and **stop their crying**."*

For the positive parent of a newborn (who, perhaps, enjoys the chaos of work and parenting), you could say something like: *"Yea, coworkers are awesome if they bring **new life**, especially if the company is still in **infancy**. But sometimes, they just end up being **helpless**."*

Again, it's about subtlety. In both cases, you subconsciously signal that you know about qualities of the experience. About infantile behaviors, about having to be a type of caretaker, about the stage of growing up and becoming self-sufficient, about dealing with dependent others. Your target might not even register this consciously, but you better believe his or her *sub*conscious mind will…

And that's what matters. You implant the seeds (words) and position the subconscious mind for penetration. You make a connection and gauge your target's reaction. If you can connect with his or her experience or 'quality' of infancy, you can begin to modify those conditions. You can subtly convince your target to do one thing over another, that whatever you say, is a good idea.

Let's say your target appears to act like a baby. Because hey, some adults act infantile—just a fact. They make a big fuss about small things, they act all theatrical, they practically huff and puff and stomp their feet. They're 'babies.' So you might say, *"you're still **crying** over that **mess**?"* or *"don't **shit** your pants"* to get him or her to go along in a more forceful way. Or maybe to soften him or her up more gently, you might say: *"can you do me a **harmless little** favor?"* or *"oh **husshh**, it'll be **gentle**, everything will be okay."*

Again the trick is to manage the stage you are targeting, in your target. Your first goal is to connect through that stage. You should use the appropriate words, but also the appropriate actions. Send the right nonverbal signals. In this stage, you obviously want to mirror caring for a newborn. So use open body language, protective body language, give easy touches, taps and caresses. Establish a non-threatening physical and emotional connection. Keep your face relaxed and your tender spots exposed. You are communicating trustworthiness, caring and compassion.

<u>Learning</u> – But not all stages are about trustworthiness, caring and compassion.
Sometimes, you have to hit the grind.

We all know the grind. You wake up, you get up, you get coffee, maybe a bite—maybe a nice meal—and then you get going. Unless, of course, you're sipping Mai Tais in a hammock in the Bahamas.

But this stage isn't necessarily about the opposite either. That is, this stage isn't necessarily about *all work no play*. It's not strictly about regimen, it's more about *learning* regimen, while still enjoying regular leisure and play. More generally, the stage is about learning. Learning that life isn't fair, that bad things happen, that life isn't always amazing, or always exciting, or always safe, or secure, or predictable, or always making sense.

So what do we do? What do we think? What do we say?

Well first we learn.

In order to permeate the consciousness of an individual in this stage, you must target the uncertainties and certainties of learning. Use language that is fair, pragmatic but also with a tinge of lightheartedness. For instance, you might be talking to an individual who is tired of doing things one way, or who feels 'stuck.' Perhaps family life is getting tiresome, perhaps this individual is learning a lot but doesn't know what to do, or where to go. It all just seems so overwhelming.

So be that guidance. Become the trusted guru, the shaman in this galaxy of experience. But also, acknowledge the craziness:

"Just take it day by day, the good with the bad, and you'll be fine. It might get crazy, but let me know."

Targeting somebody in this stage means you are targeting somebody who is largely insecure and unsure. Thus, you can sway them to do your bidding. Many men and women use these tactics to suavely convince the opposite gender to do something. With men, it's usually used to convince a woman to engage in sexual activity. For women, it is usually used to convince men to perform tasks or favors, usually accompanied with the false promise of some indeterminate sexual act.

For instance, a man might try to convince a woman to come back to his place by acting calmly, as if he has it *all* figured out. As if he can steer her away from any bad outcomes, end her fears, and show her the path: *"Come on, we'll have one more drink here, hop in my car, cruise down the road, and spend a little time at my place. No pressure, no expectations. If you wanna leave I'll call you a cab—okay?"*

So he's showing that he's the prime learner. He shows that he knows how to time it. They'll have just one more drink, not get too tipsy, but just relaxed, and then he'll drive her just down the road to his own place. He won't force anything on her, and if she feels weird, he'll pay for her transportation to leave.

A woman might target the sentiments of this stage in a slightly different way. See, a woman might show a man that she too has it all figured out, either through sexual innuendo that she wants to actually *lead* to sex, or innuendo that she doesn't want to actually lead to sex.

Let's say she recognizes a guy is attracted to her, but doesn't feel the same way about him. However, she *does* want his skills, as he can fix the problems with her car. She might say: *"I was really hoping to have my car fixed sooner than later... How about I drop my car by, and then you can just take a look at it whenever you've got free time. You know I'll make it up to you..."*

So in this case, she states that she wants her car fixed soon, but then acts casually – *"whenever you've got free time"*— but then implies she'll do something 'extra' for him if he expedites the process: *"I'll make it up to you."*

But sexual encounters or innuendos are only one tiny part of targeting this stage.

After all, you can act as if you are the 'one-in-charge' a number of ways. You can play this role at work, at home, out and about, with family, friends, acquaintances or strangers. In daily routines or unexpected events. The trick is to simply downplay the potential severity or consequence of what *you* want, and make it seem that it's what your *target* wants.

Speak about how it will affect them, be good for them, and help advance them. Rarely, if at all, mention how it will affect yourself, unless you are trying to downplay that it greatly benefits you, or unless you are including yourself under the *"we"* umbrella.

Your nonverbal communication is important too. Both men and women will use confident and assertive body language. Erect stance, shoulders back, feet evenly spaced, relaxed face, wrists exposed, and plenty of nods and instructive hand gestures, such as pointing, signaling, and representing (or visualizing) some realistic possibility. You are the guide, you are the man, woman, knowledgeable one-in-charge. So take charge. But be calm, be resolute, and make a tough situation (even if it's easy for you) seem easy for others. Even, if possible, *fun* for others.

Love-seeking – You remember what it was like to be young, dumb and in love? Well maybe not, but you do remember what it was like to date? Or maybe you're still on the market, looking for that special somebody to finally make you feel like you found the one.

Regardless of our current relationship status, we can all relate to what it's like to be attracted to someone, to have feelings that are seemingly… different. You want a lover, you want a friend, but most importantly, you want somebody to spend time with.

So what do you do?

Well, if you're like people in this stage, you go out of your way. But you're green, you're new, you're inexperienced on the scene. You mess up, you act awkwardly, you don't say the right things or send the right messages. You want to catch the attention of that special somebody but you're not good at it. In many ways, you're shooting in the dark…

This is what a person in this stage is like. So know it. See if the person you target is currently 'Love-seeking.' If so, why is that person love-seeking? What is that person doing to love seek? Is he or she confused? Is he or she foolish, head-over-heels? Or simply looking for a fling and coming up short?

Let's assume your target is weak-kneed over some guy or girl. Or let's assume your target has no romantic interest at all. That's right, let's assume that the reason you target this individual is not because this individual is actually seeking love... but because this individual displays a similar type of feverish interest in something else. Heck, it could be that this individual is seeking a new place to live, but in doing so, goes about the process with the obsessive, inexperienced, fumbling attitude of a teenager discovering the opposite sex.

Maybe this individual doesn't know which sites to go to for research, and quickly becomes hooked on one potential apartment or house, only to quickly jump to another one when it seems better. Regardless, it is clear to you that this individual is obsessively seeking new places without sound reasoning; emotion leads the way, and this individual never seems to close the deal.

So where do you come in?

Well, firstly, you can help or you can hinder. You can exploit the clueless-lover attitude or steer it in a better direction. If you choose to exploit it, you can do this a number of ways. You can be commanding, using strong, threatening body language to cut this individual off at the knees. Or you can adopt an encouraging attitude that leads the individual into making decisions you want. You might notice how the individual constantly seeks your advice. You can use this to your advantage by supplying minimal opinions until the option you want is presented.

You can be blunt (like telling a friend somebody is out of his or her league) and present the option you want from the beginning. Or, you can even further confuse the individual, offering even more options, giving contradictory opinions about a preferred option, or saying *one* option is best while recommending another. Oftentimes, telling somebody he or she can't have something, or isn't good enough for something, will make that somebody want it more. Reverse psychology. For instance, you might tell the individual that he or she shouldn't pursue *option a*, but then go on to say how amazing *option a* could be. In the end, the individual will like those positive traits and go after *option a*, leaving *option b* (the one *you* truly wanted) all to you.

Rebellion – We all rebel. Whether long-haired with a joint and no care, skipping out on work with a convenient excuse, or literally taking to the streets to make our mark, we all have the spirit of rebellion somewhere inside. It's human nature. We want what we can't have, and we always want more. We don't like being told what to do (at least not all the time), and we don't like missing out on a unique experience when life can be so rare.

Somebody in this stage—and perhaps we all are—will be noticeably against-the-grain. The individual could be young, middle-aged, or elderly. It doesn't matter. What matters is that there is a consistent effort to oppose what is considered normal or expected for that age range, social class, developmental point, etc.

This individual might be an older person who wears trendy clothes, goes out on the town, and drinks and smokes like there's no tomorrow. It could be a typical young person, choosing not to abide by the law, ignoring adults and skipping school. It could be a person with an atypical career choice, who doesn't do the 9-5 and works on an ever-changing schedule. It could be a family man or woman, who despite having that All-American family life, still finds time to play in a rock-and-roll band and live out a life-long dream.

Whatever the form of rebellion, it is your goal to target that underlining spirit and use it. You may choose to empower that rebellious energy, weaken that energy, or redirect that energy for a given purpose. Perhaps you want to divert that energy into something else. Perhaps you recognize a certain individual is very counter-culture in terms of living. He or she gets internet and cable cheaply or illegally, all furniture is purchased through obscure stores, clothes are made, meals are purchased cheaply, bills are minimized, and many a <u>health hack</u> are used to live well without spending a lot.

So use this spirit. If you want to get this individual to do something, appeal to that spirit. The trick in dealing with somebody in the Rebellion stage is to be direct, cynical, and optimistic altogether. You want to use body language that is both receptive and assertive. You are receptive to input that goes against the mainstream, but you are also assertive that you know best.

So show that you know best. Speak clearly about how you feel about things. Don't mince words. Be cynical about aspects of life and the world. Speak of *systems*. Talk about how systems can be oppressive or incompetent. How things don't work like they should, how immorality is rampant, how problems are pervasive and how most people are too distracted to notice. But also be optimistic. Remember, you rebel because you believe you can bring about a better way. You rebel because you want to change the system. You rebel because it's the best, and only, real choice.

And speaking of choice, remind your target that real choice is rare. Illusory. That you need to take the few choices inside your control and make them work.

So do so. If you want your target to feel, think or act a certain way, target the rebellious spirit. Talk about how what you want is what they want, but that they just don't know it yet. Talk about how a new method, or manner, or pathway is better. Because it's alternative, and smarter, sleeker, sharper, more cunning, more effective, than any of that nonsense in the normal world. Appeal to the inner rebel of your target (even if what you're suggesting is pretty tame) and watch what happens. If you are seasoned, you can get your target to rebel against the thing of your choosing, even if that thing is objectively mainstream!

<u>Entrenchment</u> – This stage is also called middle age.

What are the expectations of middle age? For most of us, pretty simple. We're established in a job or career, we have a family, or a partner or spouse, we have a set of friends and acquaintances, and we generally know what to expect from our daily routines. There are bills to pay, people to see, places to go, things to do, and events to attend.

Basically, we're entrenched.

But for many people, this stage symbolizes a feeling of being 'trapped.'

An individual may think, I've worked hard for years and have followed the path, and for what? For this? Is this it? What else should I do? Will I be doing this for the rest of my life? Is there anything else? Is this what people my age do? Should I change? Am I happy? Am I content? Do I even know what those words really mean?

You can tell when somebody is stuck in this stage. And it doesn't matter if he or she is middle-aged or not. A teenager could act like a middle-aged person. A 70-yr-old could act middle-aged. It's all a matter of mindset.

You may notice a quiet desperation in the way your target acts. He or she will speak as if everything is okay, but in a monotone, or saddened tone. He or she may seem uncertain, unsure, tired but wanting more.

There are several ways to penetrate the psyche of somebody in this stage.

(1) Firstly, use evaluative body language. Lean back slightly, nodding, rubbing your cheek, and scanning the face. Offer solutions or suggestions that (even if radical and emotional-based) are framed in rational, practical language. You may say, *"I concur, but..."* or *"I would suggest,"* or *"a new course of action"* or *"therefore, you should"* or *"try implementing..."*

In this approach, your role is to act as a type of life coach/guru/psychiatrist. You are calmly, clearly articulating rational responses to the malaise of entrenchment.

(2) You can also approach entrenchment with a strong, upbeat, youthful energy. Ask your target *'what do you have to lose?'* Get your target to acknowledge his or her current discontent, or longing for more, and promise to fix it. Convince him or her to leave the comfort zone, to take risk

and do something crazy. Become the voice of fun and wildness. Become the counter to your target's conscience...

"I better not, it could be a little dangero—

"Oh come on! Have some fun, for crying out loud!"

In this case, use expressive communication, exaggerated hand motions, wide facial expressions, and open, engaging body language.

(3) Finally, you can act with reverse psychology. Recommend the most boring, mundane, unsatisfying courses of action. Guide your target toward not only continuing the entrenchment, but toward becoming even more 'trapped.' Pretend to be the most milquetoast person on the face of the earth. Basically tell the target that they *have* to be entrenched. That it's the only way. This will likely steer your target toward becoming *less* entrenched. That is, less lame... like you.

Now, if you actually *want* this person to stay entrenched, you can also use the aforementioned approaches. Except, use (1) and (2) toward the opposite effect. Instead of using evaluative body language in approach (1) to take your target toward more liberated living, try this:

Take your target away from liberated living. Calmly, clearly, resolutely explain how entrenchment activities can be adaptive and productive.

In approach (2), use theatrical language to defend entrenchment and attack wilder behaviors:

"What, you wanna go out and get drunk every weekend, go on road trips like some kinda mindless college idiot? You've got beautiful kids, a nice job, a great spouse! Enjoy what you got, you can spruce it up, sure, but don't go being a clown!"

And finally, for approach (3), feel free to convince your target that being wild is the only way. That settling down is a fool's errand, and that it can't be done well, and that few people have done it well, and that your target certainly isn't one of those people. This reverse psychology will make your target want to prove you wrong—thus, becoming even *more* entrenched.

Aging – At one point or another, we realize we won't live forever. We're tired more than usual, we wake up sore. We can't move around as quickly, or think as clearly. We can't hear as well, see as well, sleep as well or go from this to that to this to that, as well. We've got a few miles on the engine and life is catching up.

We've got problems. Maybe more physical. Maybe more mental. Whatever the issue, we finally admit that we're getting old, and we're not the same sprightly young doe we once were.

What we lack in physical ability, we make up for in experience and wisdom. But we're aging, and we can deny it no longer.

So what do we do?

Well, we live. We take care of ourselves and try to keep going. But more importantly, we begin to think about the future, and how we want to spend it. What have we always wanted to do? What are our main goals? Where do we want to go and who do we want to see? And how soon till we can do it?

If you're targeting somebody in the Aging stage, you're targeting somebody who feels worn and weathered, and is looking for something more, something different, before it's too late.

Whether it's a young person who feels old at heart, and in body, or an older adult planning for retirement and trips around the globe, you know one thing: your target wants surety. Your target wants a guarantee that a certain way of life is secure, so that *new* ventures can finally be realized.

So give them that surety. Speak with confidence, keep a relaxed demeanor, be willing to listen logically with consistent eye contact and nods, occasional thoughtful strokes of the face or chin, and the much-needed clasp or pat on the shoulder as if to say, *"I understand."*

The main thing you want to do to penetrate the psyche of a person in this stage is, acknowledge. Just listen, and acknowledge. Show that you understand that life isn't getting any longer. That you recognize that decades of living have already passed, and that your target wants to achieve new goals and reach new levels, of experience.

You are a person who understands, you are a person who makes the extra effort. Relate by offering humorous examples of how sometimes you wake up with aches and pains. How you can't run around like you used to, how sometimes you feel the 'youngins' don't appreciate the finer things in life.

It doesn't matter how old you are, show patience and concern. Listen when you're not talking; signal that you're listening by delivering nod after nod. Smile and chuckle.

Now persuade. Convince. Guide your target to the conclusion you want them to reach. If you want your target to relax for a bit and not ask certain questions, or not explore certain areas (because they'd be problematic for you), then be cunning. Assure your target that new experiences will come, but that for now, the body and mind should rest.

If you want to motivate that old man or woman to action, simply point out how sitting around and rotting isn't going to improve things. Tell him or her to 'suck it up' or gently suggest the benefits of activity and effort. Remind him or her that it could be now or never, that life isn't guaranteed, that good health eventually ends, and that things should be enjoyed sooner than later.

Whatever your personal goals in approaching your target, be smart. Be measured. And always, always acknowledge the conditions that precede this stage. Bring up nostalgic days, bring up passing memories, bring up the frailty of living, bring up the regrets of age. Just no matter what you do, don't expect immediate results. Plant the seeds, time and time again, and eventually your target will think, feel and behave a certain way.

After all, time keeps on ticking ticking ticking, and what better day to change, than today?

<u>Impotence</u> – This one sounds bad already, so you probably get the picture. Think old, really old. Senile. Broken down. Alzheimer's. Dementia. In a wheelchair. Incapable of caring for oneself without a nurse or caregiver. No teeth, barely any eyesight, barely any sense of smell or taste. No hearing. No clue, really, what's going on. The body is withered, the mind is gone, and yet somehow, life continues on.

Although many people never reach this stage of life in terms of chronology, significantly more people reach this stage in a figurative sense. What's that like, you ask?

Easy. First you have to understand that some people feel totally incapable, like they've been sapped of all their energy and faculties. They may be depressed, addicted, injured, or simply at a point in their life where numerous factors are weighing heavy upon them. Whatever the reason, their psyche is vulnerable.

Now, you can do one of two things at this point. You can offer them a <u>light in the dark</u> or you can exploit that darkness, that inability, feeding into it, thriving off of it, turning it inside out.

If you choose to motivate them, and perhaps because you need their help, you can do it powerfully. Begin by showing them that they are wrong. Their reasoning is faulty. Their spirits are low.

But they don't have to be.

The human mind, you tell them, can overpower anything.

Have them do basic tasks and build progressively from there. Show them that if they can manage their crippling burden, one small step at a time, they can cast free the shackles. They can break free from the feeling that something is wrong. One step at a time, they can do it. One small step at a time.

If need be, model something yourself. Show them how *you* can do it. Heck, even act as if it's harder for you than it really is—connect with them!

Now, if you choose to *exploit* their impotence, you will take a different route. You will penetrate their psyche by reminding them that they're right. *Nothing can be done at this point. The odds are insurmountable. Potential has waned, days have fallen dark. It's over.*

There is simply nothing they can do. It might not even be their fault, you assure them, but no doubt, it is their problem.

And there is nothing they can do.

And the problem is growing. Too quickly for them to stop it. Too big for them to even fully see it. So in the end, the best thing they can do?

Give up and give in.

And who is there to takeover when everything comes undone? Why you of course. You and only you. Throughout all, you will use either firm, threatening body language (*"you better get out of your funk!"*) or warm compassionate body language (*"it's okay, I'll take care of you"*).

Be either firm or gentle. And play the part. Remember: You will watch over their things, gain control of their life, and see that goodness comes from their end.

In a sense, you hold power of attorney. Even if the target is far, far from actually dying...

But this isn't about dying. None of this is. It's about living. If you so choose to use your powers for dark results, that's your choice and one you will have to live with. But what really matters, is what you gain...

Now that your pineal gland is decalcified and activated, now that you have a firm grasp of the types of mental states of people around—now it's time to choose!

What. To. Do...

But what if you're *still* unsure? What if you don't know if it's working, if you're actually, successfully, permeating their subconscious and engaging their faculties on a deeper level?

How do you know, you ask?

Well...

It's Time to Find Out.

Brain Freeze- Knowing WHEN to Permeate the Psyche

Alpha-Theta State.

That's what you want. Alpha-Theta State.

We can do everything we want by opening our pineal glands and more deeply perceiving the thoughts, feelings, intentions and behaviors of those around us. But, the *best way* to achieve this level of higher cognition is by freezing the brain.

However, this 'freezing' of the brain doesn't mean you're actually stopping it in its tracks. Nor does it mean that you're somehow 'dumbing down,' or overloading, the brain of your target. Think of freezing food. You put it in the freezer, but it doesn't freeze right away. You gotta wait a little bit.

More than anything, freezing the brain refers to the ability to effectively transfer the brain from Alpha state to Theta State.

See, your brain is an amazing electro-chemical organ. Even when you're barely conscious, signals are zipping around your grey matter, coordinating this and that, and ensuring that everything keeps going. In Alpha state, your brain waves are moving at a slower rate than during your normal daily functioning. In Alpha state you are decidedly in the non-arousal phase. Your waves move between 7 and 14 cycles a second, and you are highly relaxed. You may even be in a mindset of meditation. Although you are extremely relaxed, you may also be extremely focused, wholly on a singular idea or entity.

Some research shows that studying and learning are optimized in the alpha state. People are able to make deeper, perhaps more abstract, connections between seemingly unrelated things. In a sense, alpha state is about allowing connections to flow, instead of consciously forcing yourself to find them and dissect them. This is why some people swear by meditative music when studying, because it engenders similar meditative brain waves.

Theta, like Alpha, signals a significant shift from the aroused waking state we all experience in our daily lives. Theta is essentially an even deeper form of Alpha. Although Theta brainwaves are most prevalent in sleep, they are also considered a conduit for learning, remembering and intuiting. Theta state represents a very internalized focus, often found in hypnosis and the rapid-eye-movement (REM) phase of sleep. In this extremely restful, inward state, our brain waves slow to 4-7 cycles per second. Many people who practice deep meditation or mindfulness strive to reach this mind-space of untouchable calmness. In the moment. In silence. In a world detached from the reality surrounding.

Theta waves are believed critical for a number of reasons. They govern our beliefs and behaviors, channel our creative energies, keep us interconnected and spiritual, and operate at subconscious levels unseen to the naked eye.

Now, getting your *own* brain in Alpha or Theta state is one thing. And cognitive training and emotive control are key. But when you want to penetrate the subconscious, permeate the psyche, of *another* brain, you need to set the stage.

So how *do* you get your target in this brain wave state?

Well, it's probably actually easier than you might think. All you have to do is engage. You want your target as relaxed as possible, and as fixated as possible, on a single idea or thought or set of thoughts. You begin this by being open in your body language, but also by partially mirroring your target to create the unconscious connection. You keep your tone of voice even, the volume soft and your facial expression easy.

You don't have to be a hypnotist or trance-inducer for this to occur. Talk about something that you want your target to be thinking about. You want them to think deeply but not in a highly aroused fashion. In other words, not fervently looking for an answer. Instead, you want them to think about it wholly and slowly, so that it consumes their being. So that they turn away from the external world, and become introspective.

Oftentimes this requires speaking of things that are more abstract or theoretical. Or simply offering a question. You may say something such as *"It appears"* or *"Seemingly..."* or *"I wonder..."* or *"You ever wonder…?"*

Try to make statements sound like questions by changing your pitch. Keep a calm, regular manner of speaking and draw attention to the fact that something is complex. Confounding. Multidimensional.

Now, this doesn't mean that the idea you plant has to be necessarily super complicated. In fact, part of inducing Alpha-Theta state is the ability to *fully* ponder what otherwise could be a simple thing.

For instance, you may choose to induce the thought of a ketchup bottle. That's right, a *ketchup bottle*. What's so cool about a ketchup bottle? Well, think about it. Have you ever really thought about it? The exact hue of the ketchup… is it darker red—crimson? Is it lighter? Has it gone bad? Is it watery or viscous? Is the bottle plastic, how plastic? How hard or malleable? How was the ketchup made, from how many tomatoes, in what way were they processed? Squeezed? Compressed and drained? Mashed together in a giant vat? Who came up with the idea of the standard bottle? Was it designed for optimal delivery? How long does it take if you just leave the…

You get the point

Whether thinking about something as mundane as a ketchup bottle or something as cosmic as the source of inter-dimensional time-space folds, the trick is to focus solely on that something. You start to imagine the smooth texture of that ketchup on your fries, the slight differences in tartness, zestiness, sweetness, and so on. You imagine the coolness in your mouth, the smell in your nose. Or with the inter-dimensional time-space folds, you imagine the theories behind it, the possibilities for infinite travel, how it came to be, how many alternate realities are existing, who's in them, what they're doing, if they're human, subhuman, partly human, far from human, and on and on and on...

This is what you want your target thinking about. You want your target to think about these things in a way that is stimulating. That means, in a manner that stimulates your mind and body in 5 critical ways:

(1) <u>Observable Physical Response</u> – the fixation embedded in your target's psyche should elicit a discernible physical response. Perhaps, flushed skin or paling of the flesh. Perhaps, the target turns a little blue or tightens or relaxes and breathes more slowly. Whatever it is, you can see it is happening, and your target may not even be aware of it.

(2) <u>Motor Response</u> – The target will move in some manner. This may be something as simple as a twitch or jerk or shrug of the shoulders, or something as heightened as a sudden and

powerful jump-up the likes of which The Hulk would be proud.

(3) <u>Sensory Response</u> – The target will experience some sort of sensory response. This one may be more difficult to determine, as oftentimes you won't know what the target is feeling. However, other physical changes may indicate the sensory changes. For instance, if the target becomes flushed, he or she may be feeling hot or tingly. If the target begins to scratch or rub, he may be feeling itchy or sore; if the target flails the nostrils, he or she may be smelling something. If the eyes widen or squint, he or she may be feeling intense light or be struggling with vision. Whatever it is, you can determine that sensory responses are occurring and affecting the target.

(4) <u>Emotional Resonance</u> – Emotional intelligence is the predictor of this behavioral response. The target will typically display a cluster of sensory, motor and physical responses to indicate a certain emotional state. Tears and flushed cheeks and curling up will indicate fear, or sadness, or helplessness. Tightening, and standing up and assuming a defensive position may indicate anger or hostility. Other times, a target may become still and thoughtful, deeply

contemplating something you've embedded in his or her mind.

(5) Thought Disparities – Oftentimes, your target may change thinking patterns as a result of your psyche permeation. This can be demonstrated through the way the target moves, such as scratching the chin or tilting the head, or just generally changing cadence. This can also be demonstrated through the way the target talks, either changing tone, pitch or speech pattern. The target may also display certain physical responses. Thoughts may not flow logically, or may come rapid-fire. The thing to notice is a sudden and distinct change in the apparent way your target thinks, and in the way he or she demonstrates that thinking.

Remember, you want your target to ultimately fixate on the seed you've embedded. So if your target is reacting more slowly or becoming still and solemn, you *may* be progressing. However, if your target is in a blind-rage, he or she is not fixated in deep thought, and Alpha-Theta state will not be achieved.

Sure, your target may *initially* display volatile emotional and behavioral changes, but the *end* goal is to achieve a relaxed state that is clearly Alpha-Theta. This state is ideal for slipping into the slipstream of subconscious energies. Individuals in this state are more thoughtful, more open, more suggestible, and ultimately more malleable.

But how do you know you've truly induced an Alpha-Theta state in your target? How do you truly know you've done your best to engage the mind and body and create an entry point into your target's subconscious mind?

Here are a number of easily observable signs your target is engaged:

(1) Change In Their Pattern Of Breathing

Simply look at the lips, the mouth, the diaphragm and the shoulders. When somebody is interested in something, they typically breathe faster. This is because they are stimulated, and interested, and feeling an excitatory state. When people are sedated, they typically breathe slower and more quietly.

You can notice the chest rising and falling, the shoulders cresting and falling, and the mouth open as the lips sometimes move as well. The nostrils may also flare. If your target is breathing slower, you are engaging Alpha-Theta state.

(2) Pupil Dilation

If you've ever seen anybody get excited, or high on certain drugs, you've noticed the pupil changes. Our pupils typically get bigger to let in more light so we can see better. This is why pupils grow when looking at somebody who we find attractive.

Pupils also dilate when we're entering a state of deep internal dialogue. This is because we are zoning out, opening our mind and body to a singularity of stimuli. This signifies the shift from conscious thought to unconscious, auto-pilot thought. The pupils increase as they defocus, unencumbered by the external environment. As research has shown, this retraction from the external world insulates the body and <u>brain from external stressors and prioritizes internal states.</u> It is also common in people who daydream frequently.

(3) Facial Symmetry

Humans are attracted to symmetry. We find symmetry in nature all the time. In snowflakes and petals and leaves and swirling patterns in the clouds or in rain puddles. We also find symmetry in our fellow humans attractive. <u>Many studies</u> indicate that asymmetrical faces are found less attractive to both men and women than symmetrical faces. This occurs for a number of reasons.

Firstly, symmetry indicates health and wellness. It correlates with a balance of biological processes, of emotional states, of thought and feeling. It signifies superior genetics and superior adaptation to environmental stressors and constraints. Faces that become warped with time may indicate maladaptive responses, abnormal mental and physical states, and deficiencies in functioning.

When your target is entering the Alpha-Theta state, symmetry increases. As the mind withdraws from the external world, external stressors dissipate. The mind allows the body to relax naturally, to let go of conscious factors that might skewer your eyebrows, or tighten your jaw, or narrow your eyes, or lopside your lips.

As the Alpha-Theta state sets in, the face lets loose.

(4) Increased Passivity

The target will typically become more passive and thus more manipulable, as the Alpha-Theta state sets in. This occurs because you are establishing an uplink with their unconscious mind. Their *conscious* mind, normally riddled with emotions, thoughts, and all sorts of responsive mechanisms, has been turned off. People who are normally uptight and anxious will talk slower, show less resistance, challenge you less, and use fewer words. You may also notice a monotone voice, which is one major indication that you have achieved Alpha-Theta in your target. The inability to control pitch and intonation is a direct result of the 'shutting off' of these normal processes.

(5) Swallowing More Frequently

Like breathing, swallowing typically slows when the target enters Alpha-Theta state. As research shows, both swallowing and respirating are controlled by many of the same muscles, and through the medullary regions of the brainstem.

Targets who are entering this stage may suddenly stop swallowing or may swallow at a much lower rate. This is because such reflexes are relaxed in the Alpha-Theta state…

(6) Stillness

Speaking of slowing and relaxing, many people in Alpha-Theta state will become extremely still, with limited mobility, if any. Just imagine a Buddhist monk, alleviating all restive attributes. The beauty of this is manifold...

When inducing Alpha-Theta state, you have essentially rendered your target immobile. You have essentially hijacked the part of the brain that controls conscious responses...What does this mean? It means you can now physically manipulate your target (if you so choose).

But more than that, it means that your target is no longer functioning in the external world. You have most likely *stopped* existing to your target, which means your powers are even greater...

(7) Skin Tone

Be observant. You may also notice various surface-level changes, such as those in the pigment of the flesh. This increased color is a result of improved circulation, which naturally occurs in healthy, relaxed organisms. However, the target may also lessen in color, becoming ashen, as blood is withdrawn from sensory organs normally attuned to the external world.

But not everybody is easily turned away from the external world. Some individuals rarely achieve Alpha-Theta state, aside from periods of extreme fatigue or when they're sleeping. Some people are simply so connected to the external world, they wouldn't know how to detach if they wanted to. That's where *you* come in.

Think of the modern world. We live in a day and age that is constantly in flux. We seamlessly connect to technology, we become addicted to cellphones, devices and screens. Attention spans are shrinking. Social media is everywhere. And our children, subject to this crazy mess, are diagnosed with ADHD like never before.

This is why it is incumbent upon you to change the game. You need to help people break from their self-reinforcing behaviors. You need to help them break the cycle.

But more importantly, you must expand their consciousness.

Imagine somebody who is constantly on his or her phone. You tell this person to get off the phone for three days, no use whatsoever. Now, the person might think you're crazy. They'll tell you that it can't be done. That they need their phone for everything, to talk with friends, to do business, to find locations, in case of emergencies—a million and one reasons why the phone is necessary.

But what if it *is* easy to break this pattern?

See, this person doesn't believe it can be done, because he or she has never done it. He or she has never *visualized* doing it.

So you plant the seed.

You mention it repeatedly. Here and there. You show up without your own phone. You nonchalantly mention how you forgot where it is, haven't used it, how you feel better without constantly being glued to it.

You implant in this person's mind the idea that not having a phone nearby is not only feasible, but better.

Reality is all that you make it. *You* can <u>become the architect of your own reality</u>, and you want your target to do the same thing too. However, what you don't tell your target, is that *you* are actually the architect of his or her reality too. *You* are planting the seeds in his or her subconscious, and as they grow, it is *your* idea that he or she will believe as his or her own.

It's all about being subtle.

Repeated, harmless, casual impressions. Don't force, don't stress. Merely drop mentions and statements, give small examples, and convey personal experiences. The trick is to make it forgettable… to the conscious mind, but powerfully imprinted on the unconscious mind.

And once you start small, you can go bigger. You can get people to break all sorts of feedback loops and 'mental prisons,' thus allowing them to experience new possibilities, take new actions, and, perhaps, do things that favor *you*.

As previously mentioned, the Alpha-Theta state allows this to happen. It allows this to happen because your target will be in a susceptible state where subconscious impressions are magnified. Your suggestions are more powerful, your casual remarks hold more weight, your statements (and commands) can literally redirect the neuro-chemistry of your target.

And if you can get your target—in Alpha-Theta—to believe that something is possible, you can get him or her to do virtually anything.

Think about alcoholics and addicts. One of the most effective programs, Alcoholics Anonymous (AA), relies on the 12 Steps. These steps are predicated on belief. Addicts are asked to believe that surrendering themselves to a higher force will allow them to change. That their bodies and minds will become a conduit for this higher force, and that despite years, decades, or even a lifetime of alcohol and drug abuse, monumental changes can occur.

Whether *you* believe in the spiritual or religious element of AA or not is ultimately irrelevant. This is merely an example of the power of belief. It shows that the neurochemistry of addicts, irreparably changed by substances, can be changed again, dramatically, for the better. Many of these addicts even put themselves in an Alpha-Theta state, meditating and pontificating on greater meanings in the World. They allow themselves to be free, open, internally engaged by ideas that were once thought impossible.

Yes, they can change.

No, it doesn't matter that they've failed every time before.

Yes, they can, once and for all, put down the drink or drug.

See, penetrating the subconscious through Alpha-Theta state does not have to result in negative outcomes. It can result in positive outcomes for everyone. Sure, it can also be used for extreme ulterior motives (ie; getting someone *hooked* on drugs), but in many cases it serves powerful, productive purposes.

What matters most, at the end of the day, after everything is said and done, is that you use your own cognitive and psychological faculties to modulate your target's cognitive and psychological faculties. This requires a multi-dimensional approach. You are quickly and effectively registering everything there is to know about the individual at hand. You are noting body language, you are noting emotional states, physical states, emotional responses, physical responses, mental abilities, likes and dislikes, preferences and aversions, strengths and weaknesses, fears and phobias, and everything else under the Sun.

But more than anything, you are noting body language and the messages contained within the accompanying non-verbal communications. You want to know what the person is saying without talking, and when they do talk, you want to know what their words are leaving out.

However, and as you know, this is rarely a walk-in-the-park.

Sometimes, with some people, it's darn near impossible to read their minds. Sometimes, you simply don't know if you, yourself, are sending the signals you intend to and want to.

Sometimes, you have to consider not only the context, but the culture, that mediates these differences.

The *milieu of body language* is critical to mastering this ancient art...

World Dominance – How to ALWAYS Send the Correct Cultural Signals

Your body is a different body in a different culture. In fact, the *cultural milieu* has so much impact on the way nonverbal communications are sent and received, that sending the wrong message could get you killed!

Well, not literally, but, uh, maybe…

Point is, there are *vast* differences across geographical divides, bodies of water, on different continents, in different countries, at varying levels of education, class and social strata—and of course, in disparate functions of written and spoken language. Knowing if no means *yes* or up is *down* is the difference between *flourishing* in various cultures and *floundering* in pathetic confusion.

Knowing cultural differences is also critical in your own culture. You might be right at home, but say you meet someone from far abroad. If you wish to mirror certain customs and habits, or show that you're well-versed in world cultures, it's best you know the body language that does so.

Of course, sometimes this can be overwhelming. Why? Because there are a *million and one* differences of body language minutiae between cultures. So let's cover some of them. Let's cover some of the most significant, those that make cultural differences immediately discernible.

These trans-cultural distinctions in communication will include those *not* previously covered in <u>Body Language Explained</u>, so if you're unfamiliar with those, please feel free to read up there for a refresher…

Tick

Tock.

Tick..

Tock...

Refreshed? Good, now let's begin:

Acknowledgment

As humans we have natural ways of acknowledging each other's presence. First we see with the eyes, or even smell with the nose. Once within a certain physical range, we further this acknowledgment with some sort of tactile experience. We may give a pat, a shake, a fist bump or something to the effect. However, we may also prefer a more detached form of acknowledgment, such as a wave or nod, often accompanied with words and expressions.

Now, for many of us, the nod is the most universal. We nod when we see someone, we can nod when someone is talking, we can nod when we want to send a signal, we can nod when we want to send a secret signal (sports such as baseball), and we can generally use the nod to indicate a number of desires, wants, moods and emotions.

But not all cultures treat the nod the same. Although nodding generally indicates approval, agreement or confirmation of some received or sent message, it sometimes can indicate the opposite of what we expect. For instance, Greeks and Bulgarians will actually nod up and down to indicate that they disagree, or that they are saying *'no.'*

Sometimes, of course, the nod is neither an affirmative or negative, it's merely a greeting. In these cases, one would think the nod's meaning is easy to interpret. However, not so fast…

See, many citizens of England and the UK will use a cross between the nod and the head shake. This quasi-nod typically has the head come down as it also twists to the side. Similar to the head nod, this head twist is a greeting as well as an abbreviated form of bowing. This gesture features a level of submissiveness, showing that we 'submit' to the other person's viewpoint (ie; agree with it).

In contrast to the head nod and head twist, residents of India use more of a wobble to indicate agreement or affirmation. Whereas Americans and Europeans commonly use this motion to indicate the possibility of agreement, in India, it represents a resolute *"yes."*

Obviously, not all head motions will indicate, signal or mean agreement. In Japan, for example, people typically nod as people do in the West. The difference is, the head nod in Japan usually means that your message has been received, not necessarily that the person receiving it agrees with you.

Visual Perception

This form of sensory input and output is critical to relations, no matter where you are on the planet. If you want to improve your interpersonal skills, increase your emotional intelligence, or simply boost your chances of success—in every facet of life—you need to know where to look. More importantly, *how* to look.

That is to say, you need to master the art of eye contact. Now, a lot of people will use various forms of eye contact for various purposes. While the persuasive powers of the third eye are undeniable, you must also learn how to use your two visible, external eyes.

Again, eye contact is key.

In the Western World, strong eye contact is used for all sorts of purposes. We do it to show connection, whether with family, friends, lovers or business partners. We do it to intimidate, to stare into somebody's mind and try to gain access to their thoughts and feelings. We do it simply to see, to note the pretty hues of another person's eyes. We do it to judge honesty and truth, to look for narrowing of the eyes, or widening of the eyes, or any indications as to what is occurring *behind* the eyes.

Eye contact in the West is stressed and emphasized for a whole slew of reasons, across a whole range of situations, circumstances and settings. In Greece, Spain and Arab countries especially, strong eye contact is preferred. Inability to maintain consistent and strong eye contact is associated with dishonesty, secrecy and weakness.

In Finland and Japan, however, eye contact is typically considered intrusive. It is believed that once a person's presence has been registered through initial eye contact, further eye contact is obsolete. Not only obsolete, but an affront to those receiving it.

In the Caribbean, eye contact is especially discouraged among younger adults, adolescents and children when being reprimanded by their parents and guardians. Eye contact during a reprimand is considered subversive and disrespectful, as it is regarded as a direct challenge to adult authority. Whereas many cultures may demand eye contact during reprimand (to ensure the children are watching and listening) Caribbean communities absolutely oppose it.

One rule of thumb is to note the geographic region of the country. If you are in the Middle East, Mediterranean cultures, Europe or and Latin American, eye contact is used all the time. If you are in northern parts of Europe or North America, eye contact is used frequently. If you are in Africa, Korea or Thailand, eye contact is infrequent. And if you are in the Far East, it is used rarely, only in those situations previously detailed.

<u>Auditory Signals</u>

Obviously, hearing is important. We don't need to enumerate all the reasons this sense is necessary, but it is important to recognize the consequences. Generally speaking, when you don't hear something, you don't respond. Your other senses may compensate, but if somebody is talking to you and you have trouble hearing, you either won't respond or you will seek alternative remedies. Failure to hear important statements, questions and commands can result in dire circumstances across the world. At the very least, it's insulting. At the very worst, you may be signing your death warrant…

But what about when the ears are not only used for hearing, but themselves manipulated? That is, touched, pulled, rubbed, scratched and fondled? In Portugal, the earlobes are actually tugged when eating savory food. By contrast, Italians will touch the ear to either indicate or <u>stimulate sexual mechanisms</u>… And in countries like Spain, touching the ear is actually a subtle way to say that a certain somebody isn't paying for his or her drinks…

The Shake

Clearly, different parts of the body represent different things. And different interactions with different parts of the body represent different things, depending upon where you are in the world. Some gestures or movements are simply not used in certain areas.

But one thing that *is* used everywhere—albeit with different meanings—is the hand shake.
The hand shake can mean everything from an innocuous *'hello, nice to meet you'* to a more sinister *'feel that power?*

I'll crush you.' What it means, and what it seems to mean, all depends on the culture you're in.

Let's review some of the most significant differences between countries and cultures:

In the United States, the handshake is typically firm. If it's loose and floppy, the person comes across as weak or untrustworthy. If it's too hard, the person seems to be trying too hard to show dominance. But a nice middle-of-the-road firm handshake is perfect. It communicates that you are confident, strong and honest. It doesn't matter if you're a woman or a man, or if the hand you're shaking belongs to a woman or man, either way a firm shake is appropriate. Five solid 'pumps' will usually suffice.

In Australia, however, women don't shake women's hands. Instead, the handshake helps to signal commonality between men and men, and men and women. Women are expected to extend the hand first, and men are expected to finish by establishing contact. This way, the act is believed to be more equitable. The woman can effectively initiate the shake on her terms, whereas the man can effectively continue and end the shake on his.

In the UK, handshakes are a quick and light intrusion, typically 3 'pumps'. This low-level invasion of space is counteracted by what you do *after* you shake hands. Upon shaking hands, individuals are expected to physically separate to allow personal space. Standing or speaking too closely is unbecoming at best, antagonistic at worst.

In Switzerland, the handshake is for *everyone*. There are no boundaries for whose hands to shake or not to shake, so when you see a person, shake hands! It is also imperative that you offer a simultaneous greeting by delivering a title. This title typically includes *Mr.*, *Mrs.* or *Miss* and the last name of the individual. Professional titles may also suffice, especially if the individual assumes a position of political power.

Romanians also love to shake hands. But only the men. Men typically only shake the hands of other men, and will do so for each and every time they greet each other. This means if you are in Romania and see the same guy 10 times throughout the work day, you might shake his hand 10 times. You will also shake the hand of every other guy you greet. Throughout a normal work day, you'll do a *lotta* shaking!

In South Korea, seniority rules supreme. It is believed that the oldest person present has earned the right to start, or not start, the sequence of shaking. An easy grip is used, as the younger person pays deference to the elder. Overall, the handshake communicates a trust and respect for the wisdom of the elder.

The United Arab Emirates has a similar hand-shaking approach to South Korea, with one key difference. Although one is expected to shake the hand of the oldest person present, the older person present does not *initiate* the shake. The younger person is expected to initiate with his or her elder, shaking for an extended period. From there, the older person ends the hand shake. Failure to hold onto the elder's hand throughout the shake represents a certain faux pas.

In Russia, hand shakes are a little different. Men never shake hands with women unless in a corporate environment or some other highly formal setting. Men are expected to show sensitivity and chivalry, kissing the woman's hand instead. Whether man or woman, shaking hands with the opposite sex is taboo.

Similar to Russians, people in Morocco only shake the hands of those who are the same gender. The hand shake is expected to be gentle and easy, as increased pressure signifies negativity. Cultural stigmas concerning gender differences forbid men and women from shaking hands.

Unlike Morocco, Mexico encourages hand-shaking. In fact, the longer the better, as this indicates a warmth, openness, and honesty of character. Men are even permitted to follow the long handshake with a hug. Women do not initiate hugs, but men are allowed to enact this more physical action, as a slight form of assertion.

Turkey also uses a long handshake. However, the handshake is expected to be soft, as excessive firmness is considered disrespectful. Interestingly, even if the shaking has stopped, one is expected to hold the hand for an extended period. Generally, the longer the hand is held, the greater the bond between individuals. Kissing of the cheeks is also practiced all over the country. Even men kiss each other on the cheeks, unless they are meeting for the first time.

In Brazil, handshakes are typically long as well. They are also firm. Handshakes should be accompanied with strong eye contact to indicate respect and understanding. People are expected to greet with handshakes *and* depart with handshakes.

Unlike Brazil, in China the length of the handshake is not as important as the firmness. One is expected to greet the oldest individual first with a grip that is light and easy. An accompanying bow is expected, as is an avoidance of direct eye contact. Using direct eye contact may result in assumptions of rudeness and hostility.

Thailand, however, doesn't care about eye contact during handshakes. In fact, they don't shake hands at all! In Thailand, people place their palms together near the chest, as if in some form of prayer, and bow. But don't go bowing right away. As an outsider to the culture, it is important that you let the other person bow first. Return the gesture when they have resumed upright position.

Dissimilar from Thailand, France is pretty easy. There are no real hang-ups or details you need to know. Simply ensure that your shake is quick and light, and be done with it. One or two 'pumps' is enough. But also be sure to offer a kiss. You want to kiss their right cheek, to your left. When they go in for the reciprocal kiss, make your right cheek available. Typically men and women exchange kisses, and women and women exchange kisses. Men and men, however, shake hands.

Of course, sometimes you wanna have a little fun. Greeting others in different cultures doesn't always have to be so regimented and boring. If you want to inject a little of your own culture, you might use a *'thumbs up'* gesture to signal that you understand. Just be sure not to use this gesture in Greece, Cerdeña or Islamic nations, as it has a very lewd connotation.

Also be mindful of using the 'OK' gesture, typically formed by touching the index finger and thumb for a circle with the three remaining fingers raised. In France, this means you are saying *'nothing'* or *'zero,'* and in Italy, Turkey, Brazil, Greece and Russia, it means you are insulting.

Another gesture to be careful with is the motioning of the finger to call somebody to you. Although this sign typically means *'come over here'* and is used with children and people with whom we're comfortable, in Asian countries, it is <u>never</u> appropriate. To many Asians, this *'come here'* gesture is used only for pets. So don't use it there, unless you want to imply an Asian individual is subhuman…

A final gesture of importance is *'The V'* known to many as *'The Peace Sign,'* wherein the middle and index fingers are spread and extended. Although widely used, it is deemed uncouth and insulting in the United Kingdom, Ireland, New Zealand, Australia and South Africa.

Most of the world, however, views this as meaning either the number *'2,'* a sign for victory, or a symbol of peace. Generally, a warm and accepting gesture of humanity.

But gestures and signs are only part of the equation. The way you shake a hand, shake your head, use your eyes and take a bow are only part of the equation. One thing many people forget to consider is distance. How far, will, you, stand… from the person?

Known as *proxemics*, the science of spatial interpersonal relations is of critical impact. Some nations and cultures believe in standing close. It symbolizes trust and respect, cements new-forming and long-standing bonds between people. These cultures and nations also believe in making more frequent physical contact. Latin America, Spain, Portugal, Greece, Italy, southern France, and many Mediterranean countries and Middle Eastern countries pride this high-level of contact. Other countries and nations, such as those of North America and Northern Europe, believe in the importance of equi-distance. They value closer speaking and occasional touching, but find increased closeness and contact intrusive, and increased distance and detachment, exclusive. In the Far East, however, distance and rare contact are considered fashionable.

In fact, the Far East views distance, and even silence, as agreeable, even receptive. Silence is considered a period of thought and consideration, deemed necessary in replying honestly and respectfully. While periods of extended silence in the Western World may be considered awkward or unbecoming, or lacking in attention or caring, the Eastern World prefers such spaces in speech.

In other words, speech is powerful to some. But the silence of wisdom may speak volumes louder...

And sometimes, we have to unlock that power. We have to go deeper. We have to move beyond the bounds of culture and society. Beyond the physical realms we inhabit, seeking something more, something stronger, something more meaningful, buried and hidden and lost within the very energy systems of our cells...

It is this energy that charges us all.

This energy, that keeps... us... *o p t i mi z e d...*

The Body of Power – Unleashing your Bioenergetics

We've all heard of therapy.

It's what gets us feeling better. Thinking clearer. Acting healthier.

It's what makes us view our problems not as walls but as platforms. Not as impassable objects, but simple potholes, minor roadblocks, necessary detours.

Therapy helps some, and doesn't help others.

But when it comes to your body, to your mind, to your spirit, you *have* to change. You have to unlock the very energies embedded in your DNA as a human of thought and conscience. You are the infinitesimal nature of your cells. You are your ancestors; you are your family. You are the amalgamation of your innumerable experiences, ideas, feelings and beliefs.

You are you. You are your mind. You are your body. You are all and one in the same. Your body is nothing without your mind, your mind is nothing without your body. The physical and the psychological create the psycho-physical. When you think something, you feel something. When you feel something, you think something.

But many of us, think, and feel, too much. Or too little. Or in ways that do nothing but complicate this tumultuous thing called Life. Sometimes, our thoughts and feelings only serve to hurt ourselves or others, or even those we care about most.

Sometimes, we are numb. Useless. Unable to do what we know, or think, or wish, we should, or could.

This is why using your body, unleashing the power of your body—and your mind—is critical.

See, body language is nothing if you can't actively balance your body and mind. If you are incapable of optimizing your body-mind symbiosis, you are incapable of truly enjoying the benefits of body language.

It's that simple.

But let's make it simpler. Let's dive right on in, to some of the top—and most effective—psycho-physical therapies known to man.

Bioenergetic Analysis:

This form of psycho-physical therapy is especially powerful because it seeks to bridge the perceived gaps in mind-body connection. In other words, it seeks *continuity* of being.

Founded by Alexander Lowen, this theory and therapy presupposes that we all carry a certain psychological state in our physical form. That is, we use physiological defense mechanisms, often unknowingly, to prime our bodies for some type of assault. Over time, these defense mechanisms shape the way we stand, move, look and feel. Many of our mental distress, health problems, and inclinations toward life stem from these early-formed psychological defense mechanisms.

In a sense, bioenergetics *create your character*.

And it is often early life experiences that make these characters stick.

Let's analyze the characters in more detail…

The Plank – Like its name suggests, 'The Plank' is rigid. It is not easily moved or swayed. It is hard and tight, marked not only by rigidity in body, form, and movement, but particularly in thought and emotion. The Plank will often adhere to outdated notions, to unrealistic expectations, and to all-or-nothing thinking in some attempt to appease impossible standards.

Most of the reason for The Plank's character stems from early rejection or neglect. Somebody close to this character was not loving enough. Was not caring enough. Was so hard and demanding and unrealistic in expectation, that now The Plank spends the rest of his or her life trying to do the impossible.

The Plank is typically perfectionist in nature. He or she may obsess over looks and body. He or she may feel highly insecure about every little unnoticeable detail. He or she may become incredibly upset, anxious, depressed or even hostile over the slightest perceived mistake or error. This can happen in everyday life, at work, in school, in relations with others—wherever. The point is, The Plank constantly worries over not being the best, and this worrying will take its toll. Because of the constant striving to be the best, The Plank is prone to exhaustion. To eventual breakdown. And often, to immune suppression. Sickness and lethargy may eventually plague The Plank, exacerbating the cycle of self-disgust and self-hatred.

In rare cases, expectations of perfection will meet harshly with imperfections of Life. In even rarer cases, suicide might become reality.

The Manipulator – This character is typically born and bred in an environment of consistent neglect, rejection and/or abuse. This character likely experienced numerous periods of harsh mistreatment. As a result, The Manipulator will become psychopathic. A facade of bravado will emerged. The Manipulator will pretend to understand the world, pretend to know things, to see things, to have everything under control. The Manipulator will develop these traits as a defense mechanism against future rejection. Thus, the false sense of confidence and control will hide a deep, penetrating insecurity.

When it comes to physical form, The Manipulator will further 'put on' for appearances. The character will stand tall and erect, even intimidating, with the eyes firm and glaring, the face impassive or smug, and the chest and abs tightened and puffed. Overall, The Manipulator will try to take advantage of others, will seek to use and abuse them *first*, so that they never have the chance to do the same.

In the end, the Manipulator will realize that he or she is doing the very thing that he or she has hated for so long. In the end, this hypocrisy of character, this flaw of nature, will tear the character in two.

The Sickle – Don't think 'sickle' like a tool or blade. Think sickle as in… *sickle cell anemia*. In other words, sickness. This character is sickness incarnate. The embodiment of disease and disorder. Typically frail, pale, and thin in body, The Sickle compensates for very early, very physical abuse. This abuse may have been corporal punishment, malnutrition, emotional torment, or isolation and alienation. Whatever it is, or was, The Sickle has learned to defend itself in several ways.

Firstly, the Sickle will hold itself as if it is ready to curl into a ball, into fetal position. It is used to being bent over, subservient. The Sickle is slumped and weary, low in energy, tight in the chest, taking shallow breaths with a fast pulse and clammy flesh. Many times the Sickle will fight his or her inner needs. The Sickle will 'press' against the body's own mechanisms, fighting against the very cells, organs and bodily systems that could help the Sickle overcome…

Why?
Simple. Because the Sickle has internalized its history of abuse. In some shape or form, the Sickle blames itself. So it fights itself. Even when it doesn't know that it is. It is rarely at ease, rarely resting, often struggling with conditions that characterize this. <u>Maladaptive responses lead to high blood pressure</u>. They lead to frequent soreness. To tingling. To eerie sensations. To phantom pains.

There might be bags under the eyes. The speech is sporadic, soft. The mind is detached. The Sickle does not seem to 'be all there.' Thoughts are scattered, moods ebb and flow, and happiness seems like something altogether forgotten.

The Addict – Similar to the Sickle, the addict is sickly in nature. The Addict is formed from early years of neglect. Proper love and compassion and care were never given. Adequate safety and security were never provided. Poor food. Poor living conditions. Poor caregivers.

The addict feels a constant void. Thus, the Addict always feels a need to fill that void. To numb the pain. To erase the memories.

In come the drugs. The alcohol. The whatever it is the Addict 'needs' to feel whole. To feel filled. To feel like something good is happening. The Addict is poor in posture, poor in muscle tone, weak in mobility, thin in build, cloudy in thought, forlorn and famished. Looking for something, anything, to heal the loneliness and embrace the spirit.

Okay.

Now that we have covered the main characters of Bioenergetic Analysis, it is time to cover the solutions. These solutions are various techniques, measures, and functional therapies that attempt to treat the core of these characters. That is, these therapies attempt to target the psycho-physical sources of these characters.

In order to correct the incorrect defense mechanisms of these characters, several things must be done. Individuals must learn to activate their bodies through various patterns of posture, movement and physical expression. The following are the most important techniques for correcting psycho-physical stressors:

Grounding – Although an ancient force that has worked for a long time, this technique has recently gained traction in the literature. Combined with new age research of body chemistry and neurochemistry, grounding is a near revolutionary act. Grounding, as the latest research shows, can drastically reduce pain, discomfort and pressure in virtually all areas of the body. This happens because grounding actually allows your natural energy to flow from the Earth through your body, actually altering the electro-chemical composition of your being.

More specifically, grounding increases the number of neutrophils and lymphocytes circulating in your system. In case you didn't know, neutrophils and lymphocytes are crucial for reducing inflammation, as they are some of the first immune system responders to sites of bodily damage. In order to ground fully, remove your shoes and socks, and either stand, sit or lay on the bare earth. Whether sand, dirt, or some other natural substance, make contact with mother nature and allow your energy system to rejuvenate.

Mobility – This may sound simple, but it's actually slightly more impactful than you might think. Simply moving about, acting out physically and physiologically, will help to trigger your tension areas. If you're tense in the arms, give some punches or make some windmills. If you're tight in the neck, roll your head or look from side to side repeatedly. Kicking your legs may also help alleviate tension in those areas. The point is to alleviate tension areas and strengthen the use of regular motion to stay limber.

Restraint – Of course, sometimes it's better not to move. Many of us have tics or habits that are unhealthy. We bite our nails, we pick our scabs, we rub our hair, we pick our noses, drum our feet or fingers and generally increase our anxiety and tension by engaging in erratic physical movements and behaviors. Sometimes, it's best to stop, and assess why the heck you're doing what you're doing.

Why are you moving like that? Do you pick because you feel some unconscious desire for self-harm? Do you feel guilty? Unable to control what's happening? Apprehensive about the future? Do you want to figuratively, and literally, run away—is that why you have 'restless leg syndrome' ? Is that why you are always anxiously moving this way and that?

Think it out and consider your problems. Why, oh why, are you acting that way?

Support – And finally, sometimes, it's best just to do what you gotta do while taking off a little steam. If you need to move this part of your body or that part of your body, do so. But do so with something in mind. Keep the other parts of your body supported. This means, rest your head a certain way, relax another area that is normally tensed or tight. Stretch it, support it on a pillow or ottoman. Use a roller. The trick is to move about one area of your body that is tense, while resting another part of your body. Activate one muscle group, and relax another.

If you are a gym rat, or want to become more involved, seek a partner. Somebody who can hold you while you stretch or workout. Sometimes, all you need to do is workout one thing while chilling on another...

Core Energetics:

Similar to Bioenergetic Analysis, this form of holistic psycho-physical therapy strives to align the human energy system by understanding, and treating, manifestations in mind and body. Founded in the 1970s by Dr. Pierrakos, this approach assumed that various impeded energy flows had detrimental effects on the human condition. Thus, by releasing the energy blockades, and permitting increased flow, we can naturally feel, think, act and *heal* for optimal living.

One of the main tenets of Core Energetics, like Bioenergetic Analysis, is the idea of grounding. The idea that you can contact the natural forces of the planet by exposing your bare appendages, senses, and ultimately your synapses, to the energy of the Universe. Pierrakos and associates found that standing upright offered the best opportunity for grounding—compared to lying down—because the upright position enabled the greatest range of movement and activity.

Of course, these movements are just the superficial manifestations of a much deeper personality core. According to Core Energetics, the core consists of three layers, each layer expelling different energy fields. These layers form each of our distinct personalities, and can manifest immediately, depending upon the situation and circumstance. The layers are:

(A) The Mask

This layer is the 'shell' that surrounds us. The face we put on for the world, going about our daily to-dos, dealing with our usual and unusual struggles, and attempting to show those around us who we *think* they want us to be. The mask generally represents what we are trying to be, but more importantly, what we are trying *not* to be.

Oftentimes, like a shell or facade, the Mask hides our true inner layers. Although our inner turmoil may often bubble to the surface (through expressions, body language, and muscular tension) we strive to make our mask convincing.

People who come across as fake or superficial or 'trying too hard' often misplace their energy in erecting a strong mask. Unfortunately, the mask does not represent who they really are, and in many cases, they hide severe and deeply penetrating problems and insecurities.

By most accounts, the Mask is a lie. A manipulation. A deception. It is not authentic, and it is not imbued with that deeper, more powerful vitality that honest, authentic people embody. Somebody with a strong mask will often seem deadened and unreal; by comparison, somebody without a strong mask will often appear to radiate a certain aura, drawing others far and wide to try to understand… what… exactly… this person offers.

(B) The Lower Self

Think lowly.

This is the aspect of the personality that, while hidden from view beneath the mask, has incredible power. The Lower Self is compatible with those aspects of our nature that are destructive, evil and ultimately negative. These are the aspects that make us want to hurt others. We try to hide the, but at times—under extreme stress, when intoxicated, in rare circumstances—they explode to the fore.

Theorists believe that this layer forms as a response to the negative forces of life. However, instead of being a powerful, positive energy that can counteract those negative forces, this layer simply exacerbates them. In other words, it's an attempt to fight fire with an even more terrible, ugly, fire. It's a response to Life's many problems that is aggressive, hostile, cruel, and unrelenting. It is volatile and violent. It does not care for the feelings of others. It does not care for expectations or norms.

And when it sporadically emerges…

WATCH OUT

(C) The Higher Self

Although this is called the 'higher' self, this layer actually resides beneath the layer of the 'lower' self. Essentially, it is the deepest layer of our personality, our being. It is, for all intents and purposes, our true core. Now, some people are dark and rotten at the core. Some people have a heart of gold. Most people, are somewhere in the middle—probably closer to 'good' than 'bad.'

But all people have this Higher Self, and all people have the potential to unleash this most powerful energy of all. The Higher Self is essentially the pulsating Life Blood inside all of us. It is bent on self-preservation, on continual growth, on finding connectivity throughout the greater Universe.

The Higher Self inside good people seeks to connect for reasons of positive power. In order to bring humans together, to find common ground, to promote love, virtue, compassion, empathy, courage, conviction, truth and honesty. The Higher Self, in good people, seeks to continue life, to better life, to strengthen the life bonds between other good people.

When the Higher Self is visible in good people, it permeates The Mask. When this happens, it is obvious. You can see this incredible force in good people. Their smile, their glow, the openness of their body language, the gentleness of their spirit, the power of their presence, the understanding of their words and actions, the glint and light in their eyes, the warmth of their heart and soul.

You will feel it at the same time that you see it. And it will bring incredible contentment, happiness and joy in your life.

Now, in bad people, this is not the case. In bad people, the Higher Self is even more nefarious than the shadow qualities of the Lower Self.

In bad people, the Higher Self seeks to eradicate all known positive forces in the World. It seeks to obliterate happiness and human spirit. It seeks to dominate, to instigate; to antagonize and destroy, to fester and spread, like a cancer, like a plague. Like death incarnate.

In truly bad people—and they are exceedingly rare—you can feel it. You can feel the cold and the dark. The emptiness in their eyes. The blood sucked from their flesh. The perversion of their expressions. The way their posture is warped; the way they stand. The way they walk. The way they seem to penetrate your heart like a stake.

And it's a terrible force indeed…

But force or no force, good or bad, weak or strong, what matters is what you do. What matters is how you navigate your energy, your layers. What matters is what you do to release the heavy blocks in your circulation of energy, in order to once and for all allow the natural vibrations of Life to flow through.

Practitioners of Core Energetics believe that this personal journey requires a systematic, step-by-step approach. You must first pierce The Mask. Doing this can be difficult, because many people in modern day life are so falsely identified with the mask, that they've forgotten who they are. They think they are something special. They think they are something unique. But in reality, they've merely allowed themselves to stagnate. They've become what they think others want to see, what they *themselves* see, and nothing more…

Piercing the mask requires understanding that you are not what you 'put on' for everyone else. It can be exhausting, debilitating, to constantly act and appear a certain way, when you know you are different. When you know it's a lie.

So many people in modern life, are made this way early in life. Especially in modern life, where <u>children are inundated with the pathology of unrestricted stimuli</u>. Where technologies shape our brains in ways we can't fathom. With effects we can't see. Through times we don't log.

Piercing the Mask often requires an ability to step back from Life's hectic, frenetic frequencies and to see what you've been missing. To embrace the singularity of solitude. Sometimes it's as simple as understanding why you create a falsehood as you do. What is your hope? To persuade others? To manipulate others? To appease others? To hide from others? To become undeniable to others?

Who are you trying to convince? Somebody else, or yourself?

Once you have identified the top reasons you've allowed The Mask to take too much control, it's time to address The Lower Self. That is, it's time to manage the potentially destructive shadow forces, swimming beneath the surface. These are the thoughts, emotions, and dangerous impulses we all try to hide or disguise. They are our ulterior motives.

Our dark upside-down version of ourselves when we lose our grasp on life and the world goes spinning.

To address the Lower Self, to temper, or channel, these powerful dark energies, we must first learn to temper, or channel, stress. More than anything, we must learn that stress—despite what we're told—is actually an adaptive response. Stress is conducive to environments. We just have to learn which environments, and in which way. Once we have an understanding of <u>the stress fallacy</u>, then we can begin to change.

But first: ask yourself… what *plagues* you?

What keeps you up at night? Is it something from your past? A deep, deep wound that you've never healed? A person you can't get over? An event in your life, or the life of somebody else, that you can't stop thinking, feeling, dreaming, about?

Do you feel guilty? Remorseful?

Are you filled with rage? Do you feel that no matter what you do, you can't change it? And does that haunt you?

Try to remind yourself that you're not alone. Everybody has this component, this layer. Everybody has to deal with inner demons. With moments where they lost it. With days and times and people, places and things that are linked to 'bad.'

You are not alone. You are not weak. You are not your past. Your past has made you who you are, but your present will make you who you become. And don't you ever forget that...

Now keep pressing. Once you have addressed these 'blockades' that allow negative energy to fester while keeping positive energy out, you are ready to progress. This newfound energy can now be rerouted to ground yourself physically and figuratively. Allow this energy to channel through your mind and body. Allow yourself to be yourself. Let your weirdness shine. Don't be afraid. Don't be bashful. Let your core energies circulate through your Lower Self and up to your Mask. Allow them to ooze through your mask, to pierce your mask, to overwhelm your mask. Allow the great deluge to break free!

But you ain't done yet.

Now that you are becoming a more authentic version of yourself (not someone else), you are ready to allow your energies to flow even further.

You are ready to transcend your mind-body connection and to architect your new reality.
In other words, you are ready to connect to your greater reality. You are ready to rise up and reach out. So connect to others. Bring positivity. Find *your reason to smile*. Engage those who are like you, show your true colors, engage those who are unlike you, show your true intentions, help if you can, meet who you can, promote life and connection, and fight the negative forces that can inhabit us all…

In order to fully embrace Core Energetics, it's important to practice a variety of techniques and exercises. Remember, you can do this by engaging in physical exercises. But the best secret of all is simply to stand. Ground energy through your feet and legs. Make literal and figurative contact with the earth, with nature, and with other human beings. With animals. With children who are young and vital. With the elderly, who though weak of flesh and blood, are stronger than all in soul and wisdom.

Engage self-massage. Use breathing exercises, such as holotropic breathing. Expand your diaphragm. Breath fast and frequently. Breath slowly and deeply. Seek emotionally resonant experiences, such as watching the sunrise, standing on the beach, running in a rainstorm, watching a powerful movie, going to a sporting event, hiking up a mountain, volunteering at a soup kitchen, attending a family event, and so on.

Take notes of your emotions. Keep a journal when you are happy, sad, or anything else. Paint, write, sculpt, meditate, run, dance, fix a car, make a video, start a daily habit that is creative and fun—find an outlet. Find an outlet for your energies and allow them to find their honest form.

You'd be surprised how quickly your regrets will wash away…

The Hakomi Method:

Similar to Core Energetics, the Hakomi Method aims to transcend both body and mind independently by establishing a transformative feedback loop through both. Conceptualized and developed by Ron Kurtz in the 1970s, this approach couples body awareness with evidence-based techniques to further the growth of the individual's solitary, and collective, psyche. In other words, this approach allows the individual to see how his or her psyche is both self-constructing, and interconnected to the world at large.

Based in Eastern philosophy, such as Taoism and Buddhism, Hakomi prioritizes the notions of mindfulness, presence, and empathic relating. Just as in Core Energetics, Hakomi presupposes that all of our unconscious, and conscious, physical manifestations—expressions, postures, gestures, movements, tics, sensations, and so on—are directly linked to our 'core' experience. Understanding this core experience of life, oftentimes subconscious, is thus integral to understanding how to improve your physical and psychological well-being.

Essentially, the Hakomi Method relies on five key principles that guide its exercises, techniques and mantras.

(1) Mindfulness

This is the ongoing state of mind in which all Hakomi is practiced. In fact, mindfulness is likely the most conducive mind-body state for any kind of restorative paradigm, of conscious-unconscious awareness. The key to mindfulness is existing in the singularity of the moment. That means, that you allow senses, feelings, thoughts, impulses and every other external influence to flow naturally through you. It's about not exerting your own influence on the external world, but allowing your natural filters to open up.

When engaged in a mindful state, you are inward focused. Mindfulness allows the mind-body to naturally subsume experiences and sensations, without unnecessary filtering or distracting. Things come and go in the moment. You do not try to attach haphazard meaning, you do not try to impinge your own preconceived notions or biases on what is happening. You merely allow. You permit. You receive. You are opening your mind to higher frequencies, and you are allowing these frequencies to unearth your most unconscious being.

(2) Organicity

Although not a new or novel idea, this concept has been lost in our convoluted modern life. Nowadays, we often ignore our natural ability to heal. We pop an Advil, we take a pill there, drink something here, use a pharmaceutical and get on with our lives.

What we don't realize, is that some of the <u>most powerful healing agents</u> are found in nature. Our body is prepared to self-heal, to self-organized, to self-maintain, given the right natural 'fuel.' All we need to do is provide the good stuff, and we can channel powers we never thought possible. This begins with <u>clean eating regimens</u>, it begins with powerful visualization and self-directed outcomes. It begins with our innate systems designed through evolutionary processes to expedite restoration and rejuvenation.

Sometimes, it's as simple as <u>absorbing the right environmental forces</u>…

(3) Nonviolence

This is not so much an exercise or technique as it is an attitude. When channeling Hakomi, you must understand that nonviolence is the most adaptive approach for change. You need to approach all of your obstacles, problems, shortcomings, pitfalls, failings and mishaps as manageable. You must learn to be constructive, not destructive. In other words, you are not destroying the negative forces, so much as you are changing them, rearranging them, altering them and relocating them.

The problems in your life, the negative things you do and have done, are a product of behavioral and attitudinal responses. They are maladaptive human responses to internal and external states. You cannot overcome these things by violently attacking them, because then you are merely violently attacking yourself.

Instead, you must approach these issues with care, with pragmatic thought, emotion and action. If you are to remove your poor decision-making and defense mechanisms, you must remove an inclination for brute force.

You cannot simply force yourself to change, without understanding what you are addressing, or how you are addressing it. You must recognize the source of your responses, target the source of your responses, and sustain a reasonable lifestyle to establish a *new* source for *new* responses.

Hakomi teaches this by allowing us all to see what we are for what we are. We are flawed beings, continuously improving, continuously capable of said improvement.

(4) Mind-Body-Spirit Integration

The Mind is more than your brain. It is the thoughts that, perhaps, science can't quite explain. It is the thought processes, the memories, the cognitive constructs, the ingrained behaviors, the automatic responses, that have come to define us. The Body, by contrast, is the body. Our physical form that weakens and strengthens. That can be beaten and damaged. That can be improved through exercise, diet and sleep. That can be worsened by drugs, poor life choices, and accidental events. The Body is tied to the Mind. If you think negatively you won't feel as good. And if you hurt your body, you won't feel or think as positively as you would if you hadn't hurt your body.

Then comes the Spirit. The Spirit is a conduit between the Mind & Body, but also between the Mind & Body and the minds and bodies *and* spirits of all other humans, beings and things. The Spirit is what cannot be readily explained. You don't have to be religious. But all of us have a spirit. Even if we merely call it an energy, or a force, or some kind of intuitive power. The Spirit is the connection we feel without ourselves and others. With person and places. It's what keeps us going in bad situations, and sometimes, dampens us in good situations. It can be strong or weak, at times, radiant or dark, at others. When something bad happens but we're in 'good spirits,' we may heal quicker. If we're in 'bad spirits' we may become worse. The Spirit is powerful, and it is inextricably tied to the Body & Mind.

(5) Unity

Speaking of 'tied' to the Body & Mind, the practice of Hakomi is one in which we can all develop powers we thought impossible. Unity makes this possible.

Understanding unity is about understanding that you are not one part. You are not your brain, or your looks, or your mistake you made just 5 minutes ago. You are not your triumphs or your failings. You are not what you did yesterday, or the mistakes you've made that you can't forget. You are not all the good things, you are not all the bad things. You are not what somebody tells you you are, or what somebody tells you you aren't.

You are *all* of these things, and more. Thus, when you work on self-development and improving yourself, you must work on the multidimensional aspects of yourself. This means addressing the many problems of your life.

Just imagine that one guy at the gym. He works on his biceps all the time, but neglects his other muscle groups. What happens? Well, for starters, he looks funny as heck. He might also suffer physical problems, as he is forced to overcompensate for deficiencies *he* created. So then what? Well, in time, he might continue to neglect the rest of his body, creating further problems, causing psychological distress as well, possibly exacerbating the pre-existing mental conditions that drove him to obsess over his biceps, and *only* his biceps, in the first place.

Or how about people who swear by one or two 'miracle cures'? Sure, these items or products might be powerful and effective, but what happens over time? If the individual continues to use, and overuse, these products, then the body and mind may respond negatively. Or how about with dieting? Sure, eating certain vegetables is great, but if you eat too many, while not consuming other foods, you'll have problems. You may become constipated. Your body may be screaming for grains or meat. Your body will adapt by drawing vitamins, minerals and nutrients from some parts to fuel other parts. You might feel strong in one way, but incredibly weak in another.

The point is, life is about balance. It's about Unity. And if you are unified, balanced, and at least *attempting* to target all the facets of your life, then you're on the right track…

But in order to stay on that track, you've gotta do more. You must embrace a number of important steps, to keep moving. Forwards, not backwards, in this thing called Life.

According to the tenets of Hakomi:

First you must "Contact" your critical physical and mental space. This means tapping into mindfulness. In order to enter this special place, you have to first engage a safe, comfortable, and conducive environment. This might be a quiet park bench. Your basement. An attic. A walk in the woods. A secluded beach. In a room away from others. Or maybe even in a coffee shop loaded with people where the chatter can become a pleasant backdrop to your inward dialogue...

It's all about feeling safe, and feeling trustworthy. When you are relaxed and trusting, you bring down your guard, you allow natural stimuli to arrive unfiltered, and you embrace the positive vulnerability that is mindfulness...

The next step on the track is "Accessing" which denotes the ability to essentially allow mindfulness to, well, do its thing. Basically, it's about permitting the free flow of stimuli, whether thoughts, memories, sensations, feelings, or intrusive emotions, to enter and leave unabated.

Become like a gateway where all these things come and go. In many ways you are not doing anything with them. But they are certainly doing something, however subtly, to you. You will find that over time, mindfulness allows you to "access" new understandings. By not attaching meanings or labels to these 'things' that pass through you, you'll come to understand...

It doesn't matter!!

For many of the things that worried you, bothered you, *ruined* you, you'll realize… Why??
In this way, you will learn from your subconscious. You will comprehend that you can easily change just by not reacting, or changing your reaction, to these many 'things.'

And that's all they are. They are 'things' They are nothing, they are something. They are whatever the heck you want them to be, because it is up to you to let them be. You can be extremely bothered by all of it, or unmoved by most of it. You can't make a mountain out of a molehill or you can turn a mountain *to* a molehill. Or you can say, *'screw the mountain, forget the molehill,'* I… don't… Care.

Try experimenting with various self-affirmations or self-declarations. Be complimentary, be deprecating. Tell yourself that you are a strong person. Tell yourself that you are a weak, inferior person. How do you react to either or both? Do you feel better when you say you are strong or do you wave it off as b.s.? Do you feel bad when you tell yourself you are weak? What if you imagine it coming from somebody else? Does that bother you? Does it fuel you? Does it make you more or less likely to change?

And why?

What's at your core? What's the reason for this? Why are you acting this way? What are your core self-beliefs? Where did they come from? Where were they developed? And why? By who? For whom?

Once you have thoroughly explored these thought processes, it's time to take the next step. The next track on your trek is "Processing."

This step requires that you further examine your distinct experiences and reactions. Instead of obsessing over every reason for why you do the things the way you do them, replace them. Substitute new ideas and reasons. Do what feels true to your body, mind and spirit. Seek your own personal truth. Explore your own personal landscape of morality and rationality. Don't think in terms of what others think or thought, or what others did and do. Do what you do, try new things, embrace change, accept failure, and seek success. In "Processing," the key is that it is a process. You are going through the work, you are taking in new experiences, undergoing new responses, and creating new environments.

Finally, after finding a process that feels true to who you are at your core, it is time for "Integration."

What is integration? Integration is all about looking back and moving forward. You move forward with what you've created and become, while understanding *how* you've created what you've become.

Understand how you can change moving forward. Realize that mindfulness allows you to open yourself to your inner subconscious. Recognize that your body will tell you how you react to certain things, that your mind will follow suit, that your spirit will feel the deeper frequencies of your existence.

And whatever you do, keep pressing. Keep working. And never stop becoming, the better version you know you seek...

***

In the end, it's all bout changing. It's all about constant change. As they say, the only constant in life *is* change. If you're afraid to change, you're afraid to grow. And if you don't grow, you'll never know what you could be. You'll stagnate. You stay at rest. You'll atrophy. You'll stop and tire, and eventually, you'll wither away.

This is what happens.

This is why Body Language and non-verbal communication are so important. Because at the end of the day, it's not about healing depression, or removing mental illness, catapulting your career, or meeting your lifelong partner, or strengthening interpersonal relationships, or succeeded in cultures across the world, or opening new doors for friendship, and family relations, and business skills, and sexual prowess, and general daily functioning…

In the end, all of these things are just outcomes.

What matters first and foremost, is the catalyst for those outcomes. The source.

And that's *you*.

If *you* can understand *you*, if you can change you, then all of these other things *will* follow.

If you can change you, then others will change with you. You will change others. In many ways, you won't even know it. You'll revolutionize the way you see the world. You'll alter your perceptions. You'll signal signals you didn't even know existed.

Mastering the primordial power of Body Language and Nonverbal Communication is about utilizing something that is so influential, yet subtle, so unconscious, yet unpracticed, that it will *change you forever*.

And believe you me. Once you've harnessed these powers for the betterment of *you*, you'll never look at Life or The World the same way again...

A Special Note:

Thank you for reading "*Body Language MASTERED: How to Dominate Modern Life with Primal Powers*" If you enjoyed reading this book and would like to be included on an email list for when similar content is available, feel free:

SUBSCRIBE

As always, thank you for reading. And may you continue to live healthily and happily.

Sincerely,

C.K. Murray

Other works by C.K. Murray:

1. Mindfulness Explained: The Mindful Solution to Stress, Depression, and Chronic Unhappiness

2. Emotional Intelligence Explained: How to Master Emotional Intelligence and Unlock Your True Ability

3. [The Confidence Cure: Your Definitive Guide to Overcoming Low Self-Esteem, Learning Self-Love and Living Happily](#)

4. [Let Love Flourish: The Secret to Finding Your Kindred Heart](#)

5. [Hair Loss Explained: Natural Solutions for Hair Loss and Premature Balding](#)

6. [The Omega Factor: 20 SUPERCHARGED Omega-3 Recipes for the Body and Mind](#)

7. [A Reason to Smile: Finding Happiness in Life's Little Moments](#)

8. [Health Hacks: 46 Hacks to Improve Your Mood, Boost Your Performance, and Guarantee a Longer, Healthier,](#)

More Vibrant Life

9. *Depression, Drugs, & the Bottomless Pit: How I found my light amid the dark*

10. *The Stress Fallacy: Why Everything You Know Is WRONG*

11. *Master Mind: Unleashing the Infinite Power of the Latent Brain*

12. *Sex Science: 21 SIZZLING Secrets That Will Transform Your Bedroom into a Sauna*

13.Sex Secrets: How to Conquer the Power of Sexual Attraction

14.Master of the Game: A Modern Male's Guide to Sexual Conquest

15.Persuasion Explained: How to Use Your Inner Eye to Influence Others

16.Deep Sleep: 32 Proven Tips for Deeper, Longer, More Rejuvenating Sleep

17. Win Back Your Ex! The Secrets to Rekindling Your Relationship

18._The Blood Pressure Diet: 30 Recipes Proven for Lowering Blood Pressure, Losing Weight, and Controlling Hypertension_

19._Coconut Oil Cooking: 30 Delicious and Easy Coconut Oil Recipes Proven to Increase Weight Loss and Improve Overall Health_

20._High Blood Pressure Explained: Natural, Effective, Drug-Free Treatment for the "Silent Killer"_

21._The Wonders of Water: How H2O Can Transform Your Life_

22. *INFUSION: 30 Delicious and Easy Fruit Infused Water Recipes for Weight Loss, Detox, and Vitality*

23. *The Ultimate Juice Cleanse: 25 Select Juicing Recipes to Optimize Weight Loss, Detox and Longevity*

24. *ADHD Explained: Natural, Effective, Drug-Free Treatment For Your Child*

25. *Confidence Explained: A Quick Guide to the Powerful Effects of the Confident and Open Mind*

26._How to Help an Alcoholic: Coping with Alcoholism and Substance Abuse_

27._Vitamin D Explained: The Incredible, Healing Powers of Sunlight_

28._Last Call: Understanding and Treating the Alcoholic Brain (A Personal and Practical Guide)_

29._Hooked: Life Lessons of an Alcoholic and Addict (How to Beat it Before it Beats YOU)_

30. _Fragmented: Piecing Together the Mind of an Addict_

31.Neuro-Linguistic Programming Explained: Your Definitive Guide to NLP Mastery

32.Hooking Up: A College Guy's Guide to Wild Fun, Casual Sex, and Campus Companionship

33.Natural Weight Loss: PROVEN Strategies for Healthy Weight Loss & Accelerated Metabolism

34. BEAT The Hangover: Your Ultimate Guide to Drinking, Partying and Waking up Hangover Free

35. DOMINATE - How Psychopaths Think, Act and Succeed

36. MIND SHIFT - The Key to Erasing Negative Thoughts and Unlocking Positive Perception

37. "Give it to me, Baby" - The Secret to Giving ANY Woman the Orgasmic Sex She Craves

38. No More - How to Tackle Procrastination with Power & Proficiency

39. Body Language Explained: How to Master the Power of the Unconscious

40. The Success Quotient: How to Capitalize on YOUR OWN Hidden Formula

41. Silver Magic: How Colloidal Silver Can TRANSFORM Your Life

Printed in Great Britain
by Amazon